A. J. LIEBLING

A. J. LIEBLING

THE SWEET SCIENCE AND OTHER WRITINGS

The Sweet Science
The Earl of Louisiana
The Jollity Building
Between Meals
The Press

THE LIBRARY OF AMERICA

Library of Congress Control Number: 2008934338
ISBN 978-1-59853-040-7

First Printing
The Library of America—191

PETE HAMILL

IS THE EDITOR OF THIS VOLUME

A. J. Liebling's
The Sweet Science and Other Writings
is published with support from

THE GEOFFREY C. HUGHES FOUNDATION

and will be kept in print by its gift to
the Guardians of American Letters Fund,
established by The Library of America
to ensure that every volume in the series
will be permanently available.

Contents

THE SWEET SCIENCE

To Whitey, Freddie, and Charlie, my Explainers

CONTENTS

Introduction

"Sweet Science of Bruising!"
Boxiana, 1824

"I had heard that Ketchel's dynamic onslaught was such it could not readily be withstood, but I figured I could jab his puss off. . . . I should have put the bum away early, but my timing was a fraction of an iota off."
—*Philadelphia Jack O'Brien, talking, in 1938, about something that had happened long ago.*

It is through Jack O'Brien, the *Arbiter Elegantiarum Philadelphiae,* that I trace my rapport with the historic past through the laying-on of hands. He hit me, for pedagogical example, and he had been hit by the great Bob Fitzsimmons, from whom he won the light-heavyweight title in 1906. Jack had a scar to show for it. Fitzsimmons had been hit by Corbett, Corbett by John L. Sullivan, he by Paddy Ryan, with the bare knuckles, and Ryan by Joe Goss, his predecessor, who as a young man had felt the fist of the great Jem Mace. It is a great thrill to feel that all that separates you from the early Victorians is a series of punches on the nose. I wonder if Professor Toynbee is as intimately attuned to his sources. The Sweet Science is joined onto the past like a man's arm to his shoulder.

I find it impossible to think that such a continuum can perish, but I will concede that we are entering a period of minor talents. The Sweet Science has suffered such doldrums before, like the long stretch, noted by Pierce Egan, the great historian of Boxiana, between the defeat of John Broughton in 1750 and the rise of Daniel Mendoza in 1789, or the more recent Dark Age between the retirement of Tunney in 1928 and the ascension of Joe Louis in the middle thirties. In both periods champions of little worth succeeded each other with the rapidity of the emperors who followed Nero, leaving the public scarce time to learn their names. When Louis came along he knocked out *five* of these world champions—Schmeling, Sharkey, Carnera, Baer, and Braddock, the last of whom happened to be holding the title when Louis hit him. A decade later he knocked out

Jersey Joe Walcott, who nevertheless won the title four years afterward. His light extended in both directions historically, exposing the insignificance of what preceded and followed.

It is true there exist certain generalized conditions today, like full employment and a late school-leaving age, that militate against the development of first-rate professional boxers. (They militate also against the development of first-rate acrobats, fiddlers, and *chefs de cuisine*.) "Drummers and boxers, to acquire excellence, must begin young," the great Egan wrote in 1820. "There is a peculiar *nimbleness* of the *wrist* and exercise of the shoulder required, that is only obtained from growth and practice." Protracted exposure to education conflicts with this acquisition, but if a boy has a true vocation he can do much in his spare time. Tony Canzoneri, a very fine featherweight and lightweight of the thirties, told me once, for example, that he never had on a boxing glove until he was eight years old. "But of course I had done some street fighting," he said to explain how he had overcome his late start. Besides, there are a lot of unblighted areas like Cuba and North Africa and Siam that are beginning to turn out a lot of fighters now.

The immediate crisis in the United States, forestalling the one high living standards might bring on, has been caused by the popularization of a ridiculous gadget called television. This is utilized in the sale of beer and razor blades. The clients of the television companies, by putting on a free boxing show almost every night of the week, have knocked out of business the hundreds of small-city and neighborhood boxing clubs where youngsters had a chance to learn their trade and journeymen to mature their skills. Consequently the number of good new prospects diminishes with every year, and the peddlers' public is already being asked to believe that a boy with perhaps ten or fifteen fights behind him is a topnotch performer. Neither advertising agencies nor brewers, and least of all the networks, give a hoot if they push the Sweet Science back into a period of genre painting. When it is in coma they will find some other way to peddle their peanuts.

In truth the kind of people who run advertising agencies and razor-blade mills have little affinity with the Heroes of Boxiana. A boxer, like a writer, must stand alone. If he loses he cannot call an executive conference and throw off on a vice

president or the assistant sales manager. He is consequently re-
sented by fractional characters who cannot live outside an organization. A fighter's hostilities are not turned inward, like a
Sunday tennis player's or a lady M.P.'s. They come out naturally with his sweat, and when his job is done he feels good
because he has expressed himself. Chain-of-command types,
to whom this is intolerable, try to rationalize their envy by
proclaiming solicitude for the fighter's health. If a boxer, for
example, ever went as batty as Nijinsky, all the wowsers in the
world would be screaming "Punch-drunk." Well, who hit
Nijinsky? And why isn't there a campaign against ballet? It gives
girls thick legs. If a novelist who lived exclusively on apple-
cores won the Nobel Prize, vegetarians would chorus that the
repulsive nutriment had invigorated his brain. But when the
prize goes to Ernest Hemingway, who has been a not particularly evasive boxer for years, no one rises to point out that the
percussion has apparently stimulated his intellection. Albert
Camus, the French probable for the Nobel, is an ex-boxer,
too.

I was in the Neutral Corner saloon in New York a year or so
ago when a resonant old gentleman, wiry, straight, and white-
haired, walked in and invited the proprietors to his ninetieth
birthday party, in another saloon. The shortly-to-be nonage-
narian wore no glasses, his hands were shapely, his forearms
hard, and every hair looked as if, in the old water-front phrase,
it had been drove in with a nail. On the card of invitation he
laid on the bar was printed:

Billy Ray
Last surviving Bare Knuckle Fighter

The last bare-knuckle fight in which the world heavyweight
championship changed hands was in 1882. Mr. Ray would not
let anybody else in the Neutral buy a drink.

As I shared his bounty I thought of all his contemporary
lawn-tennis players, laid away with their thromboses, and the
golfers hoisted out of sand pits after suffering coronary occlu-
sions. If they had turned in time to a more wholesome sport, I
reflected, they might still be hanging on as board chairmen
and senior editors instead of having their names on memorial
pews. I asked Mr. Ray how many fights he had had and he

said, "A hundert forty. The last one was with gloves. I thought the game was getting soft, so I retired."

When I was last in Hanover, New Hampshire, faculty members were dropping on the tennis courts so fast that people making up a doubles party always brought along a spare assistant professor.

This discussion of the relative salubrity of the Sweet Science and its milksop succedanea is what my friend Colonel John R. Stingo would call a labyrinthian digression.

It is because of the anticipated lean aesthetic period induced by television that I have decided to publish this volume now. The transactions narrated in it happen to comprise what may be the last heroic cycle for a long time. The Second World War, which began to affect American boxing when the draft came along in 1940, stopped the development of new talent. This permitted aging prewar boxers like Joe Louis and Joe Walcott to maintain their dominance longer than was to be expected under normal conditions. By the late forties, when the first few postwar fighters were beginning to shine, television got its thumb on the Old Sweetie's windpipe, and now there are no clubs to fight in. But in between these catastrophes Rocky Marciano appeared out of the shoe-manufacturing town of Brockton, Massachusetts, and Sandy Saddler, the pikelike featherweight, out of Harlem. Randy Turpin looked, briefly, like the first Heroic British fighter since Jimmy Wilde. Marcel Cerdan made an unforgettable impression before his premature death in an airplane accident. (He is not in this book, because he died too soon.) Archie Moore, a late-maturing artist, like Laurence Sterne and Stendhal, illuminated the skies with the light of his descending sun, and Sugar Ray Robinson proved as long-lasting as he had been precocious—a tribute to burning the candle at both ends.

It was in June of 1951 that it occurred to me to resume writing boxing pieces, and that was only four months before Marciano, then an impecunious, or "broken," fighter, arrived, as narrated early in this volume. There was no particular reason that I came back to boxing—"Suddenly it came to me," like the idea to the man in the song who was drinking gin-and-water. It was the way you take a notion that you would like to see an old sweetheart, which is not always the kind of notion to act on.

I had written a number of long boxing pieces for the *New Yorker* before 1939, but I dropped them then, along with the rest of what Harold Ross used to call "low-life," in order to become a war correspondent. Low-life was Ross's word for the kind of subject I did best.

When I came back from the war in 1945 I wasn't ready to write about the Sweet Science, although I continued to see fights and to talk with friends in Scientific circles. I became a critic of the American press, and had quite a lot of fun out of it, but it is a pastime less intellectually rewarding than the study of "milling," because the press is less competitive than the ring. Faced with a rival, an American newspaper will usually offer to buy it. This is sometimes done in Scientific circles, but is not considered ethical. Besides, the longer I criticized the press, the more it disimproved, as Arthur MacWeeney of the *Irish Independent* would put it.

My personal interest in La Dolce Scienza began when I was initiated into it by a then bachelor uncle who came east from California when I was thirteen years old, which was in 1917. He was a sound teacher and a good storyteller, so I got the rudiments and the legend at the same time. California, in the nineties and the early 1900s, had been headquarters: Corbett, Choynski, Jeffries, Tom Sharkey, Abe Attell, and Jimmy Britt were Californians all, and San Francisco had been the port of entry from Australia, which exported the Fitzsimmonses and Griffos. Uncle Mike could talk about them all. After my indoctrination I boxed for fun whenever I had a chance until I was twenty-six and earning sixty-three dollars a week as a reporter on the Providence *Journal and Evening Bulletin.* I continued to box occasionally for many years more, generally just enough to show I knew what was all about it, as the boys say. I went shorter rounds every time. The last was in about 1946, and the fellow I was working with said he could not knock me out unless I consented to rounds longer than nine seconds.

When I returned to the realms of higher intellection in 1951 Joe Louis was entering his eighteenth year as the most conspicuous ornament of the "fancy"—the highest feather in its hat. Within a few months Marciano appeared. This began a new cycle: Marciano and the Old Men, like Louis and the Old Men in 1934–38. During the immediately subsequent episodia, to borrow a word from Colonel Stingo, Marciano knocked out three world's heavyweight champions, Louis, Walcott and Ezzard Charles, and wound up beating Moore, the heavyweight-light-heavyweight, who challenged for the title at thirty-nine. Marciano was then himself thirty-one, which was a fairly advanced age for a boxer, but all his big fights have been against men still older, because nobody was coming up behind him. With the Moore fight on September 16, 1955, the cycle was complete. It is certain that neither Hero will ever be better than on that night, and highly improbable that either will be again that good.

All the Heroic transactions recorded within this book thus occurred within the four-and-a-fraction years, June, 1951–September, 1955, and they have a kind of porous unity, like the bound volumes of *Boxiana* Egan used to get out whenever he figured he had enough magazine pieces about the ring of his day to fill a book. There is as main theme the rise of Marciano, and the falls of everybody who fought him, and there are subplots, like the comeback of Sugar Ray after his downfall before Turpin, and his re-downfall before Maxim, but not his current re-comeback. There is some discussion of the television matter, and there are exploits of minor Heroes like Sandy Saddler, the featherweight champion, and a lot of boys you never heard of. The characters who hold the book, and the whole fabric of the Sweet Science together, are the trainer-seconds, as in Egan's day.

Egan, to whom I refer so often in this volume, was the greatest writer about the ring who ever lived. Hazlitt was a dilettante who wrote one fight story. Egan was born probably in 1772, and died, certainly, in 1849. He belonged to London, and no man has ever presented a more enthusiastic picture of all aspects of its life except the genteel. He was a hack journalist, a song writer, a conductor of puff-sheets and, I am inclined to suspect, a shakedown man. His work affords internal evidence that he was self-educated; if he wasn't he had certainly found a funny schoolmaster. In 1812 he got out the first paperbound installment of *Boxiana; or Sketches of Ancient and Modern Pugilism; from the days of Broughton and Slack to the Heroes of the Present Milling Aera*. For years before that he had been writing about boxing for a sporting magazine called the *Weekly*

Despatch. The unparalleled interest in the Sweet Science aroused by the two fights between Tom Cribb, the Champion, and Tom Molyneaux, an American Negro, in 1811, inspired Egan to launch a monthly publication confined to milling.

He covered the historical portion of his self-assigned program in his first few numbers, and after that *Boxiana* became a running chronicle of the Contemporary Milling Aera. As the man with the laurel concession, he became a great figure in the making of matches, the holding of stakes, the decision of disputes, the promotion of banquets, and all the other perquisites of eminence.

"In his particular line, he was the greatest man in England," a memorialist wrote of him long after his death. "In the event of opposition to his views and opinions, he and those who looked up to him had a mode of enforcing authority which had the efficacy without the tediousness of discussion, and 'though,' says one who knew him, 'in personal strength far from a match for any sturdy opponent, he had a courage and vivacity in action which were very highly estimated both by his friends and foes.' . . .

"His peculiar phraseology, and his superior knowledge of the business, soon rendered him eminent beyond all rivalry and competition. He was flattered and petted by pugilists and peers: his patronage and countenance were sought for by all who considered the road to a prizefight the road to reputation and honor. Sixty years ago [that would have been 1809], his presence was understood to convey respectability on any meeting convened for the furtherance of bull-baiting, cock-fighting, cudgelling, wrestling, boxing, and all that comes within the category of 'manly sports.' If he 'took the chair,' success was held as certain in the object in question. On the occasions of his presence he was accompanied by a 'tail,' if not as numerous, perhaps as respectable as that by which another great man was attended, and certainly, in its way, quite as influential."

Egan brought out his first bound volume, comprising sixteen numbers, in 1813, although the title page reads 1812. (It had gone to the subscribers with the first installment.) He did not put out another bound volume until 1818. There was a third in 1821, a fourth in 1824, and a fifth in 1828. By that time the Sweet Science was entering one of its periodic declines.

Too many X (Egan's way of writing crooked) fights had dis-
gusted backers and bettors, and there was a lack of exciting
new talent. The Science was not to reach another peak until
the rise of Tom Sayers, in the late 1850s, which would culmi-
nate in Tom's great fight with the American, John C. Heenan,
in 1860. Egan abandoned *Boxiana* after the 1828 volume.

A great charm of *Boxiana* is that it is no mere compilation of
synopses of fights. Egan's round-by-round stories, with ringside sidelights and betting fluctuations, are masterpieces of
technical reportage, but he also saw the ring as a juicy chunk
of English life, in no way separable from the rest. His accounts
of the extra-annular lives of the Heroes, coal-heavers, water-
men, and butchers' boys, are a panorama of low, dirty, happy,
brutal, sentimental Regency England that you'll never get from
Jane Austen. The fighter's relations with their patrons, the
Swells, present that curious pattern of good fellowship and
snobbery, not mutually exclusive, that has always existed
between Gentleman and Player in England, and that Australi-
ans, Americans, and Frenchmen equally find hard to credit.
Egan is full of anecdotes like the one about the Swell and his
pet Hero, who were walking arm-in-arm in Covent Garden
late one night, when they saw six Dandies insulting a woman.
Dandies were neither Gentleman nor Players, and Egan had
no use for them. The Swell remonstrated with the Dandies
and one of them hit him. The Swell then cried, "Jack Martin,
give it them," and the Hero, who was what we today would
call a light-heavyweight, knocked down the six Dandies. From
Egan's narrative it is impossible to tell which performance he
considered more dashing, the Swell's or the Hero's.

That particular Hero, by the way, was known as the Master
of the Rolls, because he was by trade a baker. "Martin is very
respectably connected," Egan wrote, "and, when he first commenced prize pugilist, he had an excellent business as a baker;
but which concern he ultimately disposed (or got rid) of, in
order, it seems, to give a greater scope to his inclinations."
Egan's cockney characters, and his direct quotes of how they
talked, were a gift to Dickens, who, like every boy in England,
read the author of *Boxiana*. In the New York Public Library
catalogue there is listed a German monograph, circa 1900, on

Egan's influence on Dickens, but I know of no similar attempt at justice in the English language.

Egan's pageant scenes of trulls and lushes, toffs and toddlers, all setting off for some great public, illegal prize-fight, are written Rowlandson, just as Rowlandson's print of the great second fight between Cribb and Molyneaux is graphic Egan. In the foreground of the picture there is a whore sitting on her gentleman's shoulders the better to see the fight, while a pickpocket lifts the gentleman's reader (watch). Cribb has just hit Molyneaux the floorer, and Molyneaux is falling, as he has continued to do for a hundred and forty-five years since. He hasn't hit the floor yet, but every time I look at the picture I expect to see him land. On the horizon are the delicate green hills and the pale blue English sky, hand-tinted by old drunks recruited in kip-shops (flophouses). The prints cost a shilling colored. When I look at my copy I can smell the crowd and the wildflowers.

Egan could be stately when he wanted, as you can see from the following sample taken from the dedication of the first volume of *Boxiana*:

To those, Sir, who prefer *effeminacy* to hardihood—assumed *refinement* to rough *Nature*—and whom a *shower of rain* can terrify, under the alarm of their polite frames, suffering from the unruly elements—or would not mind Pugilism, if BOXING was not so shockingly vulgar—the following work can create no interest whatever; but to those persons who feel that Englishmen are not automatons . . . Boxiana will convey amusement, if not information . . .

I can think of nothing more to say in favor of the Present Extension of the GREAT HISTORIAN's Magnum Opus.

A. J. LIEBLING
Paris, 1956

The Big Fellows

BOXING WITH THE NAKED EYE

WATCHING a fight on television has always seemed to me a poor substitute for being there. For one thing, you can't tell the fighters what to do. When I watch a fight, I like to study one boxer's problem, solve it, and then communicate my solution vocally. On occasion my advice is disregarded, as when I tell a man to stay away from the other fellow's left and he doesn't, but in such cases I assume that he hasn't heard my counsel, or that his opponent has, and has acted on it. Some fighters hear better and are more suggestible than others—for example, the pre-television Joe Louis. "Let him have it, Joe!" I would yell whenever I saw him fight, and sooner or later he would let the other fellow have it. Another fighter like that was the late Marcel Cerdan, whom I would coach in his own language, to prevent opposition seconds from picking up our signals. "*Vas-y, Marcel!*" I used to shout, and Marcel always *y allait.* I get a feeling of participation that way that I don't in front of a television screen. I could yell, of course, but I would know that if my suggestion was adopted, it would be by the merest coincidence.

Besides, when you go to a fight, the boxers aren't the only ones you want to be heard by. You are surrounded by people whose ignorance of the ring is exceeded only by their unwillingness to face facts—the sharpness of your boxer's punching, for instance. Such people may take it upon themselves to disparage the principal you are advising. This disparagement is less generally addressed to the man himself (as "Gavilan, you're a bum!") than to his opponent, whom they have wrong-headedly picked to win. ("He's a cream puff, Miceli!" they may typically cry. "He can't hurt you. He can't hurt nobody. Look—slaps! Ha, ha!") They thus get at your man—and, by indirection, at you. To put them in their place, you address neither them nor their man but your man. ("Get the other eye, Gavilan!" you cry.) This throws them off balance, because they haven't noticed anything the matter with either eye. Then, before they can think of anything to say, you thunder, "Look at that eye!" It doesn't much matter whether or not the man has been hit in the eye; he will be. Addressing yourself to the fighter when you want somebody else to hear you is a parliamentary device, like "Mr. Chairman . . ." Before television, a prize-fight was to a New Yorker the nearest equivalent to the New England town meeting. It taught a man to think on his seat.

Less malignant than rooters for the wrong man, but almost as disquieting, are those who are on the right side but tactically unsound. At a moment when you have steered your boxer to a safe lead on points but can see the other fellow is still danger-ous, one of these maniacs will encourage recklessness. "Finish the jerk, Harry!" he will sing out. "Stop holding him up! Don't lose him!" But you, knowing the enemy is a puncher, protect your client's interests. "Move to your left, Harry!" you call. "Keep moving! Keep moving! Don't let him set!" I sometimes finish a fight like that in a cold sweat.

If you go to a fight with a friend, you can keep up unilateral conversations on two vocal levels—one at the top of your voice, directed at your fighter, and the other a running *exper-tise* nominally aimed at your companion but loud enough to reach a modest fifteen feet in each direction. "Reminds me of Panama Al Brown," you may say as a new fighter enters the ring. "He was five feet eleven and weighed a hundred and eight-een pounds. This fellow may be about forty pounds heavier and a couple of inches shorter, but he's got the same kind of neck. I saw Brown box a fellow named Mascart in Paris in 1927. Guy stood up in the top gallery and threw an apple and hit Brown right on the top of the head. The whole house started yelling, 'Finish him, Mascart! He's groggy!'" Then, as the bout begins, "Boxes like Al, too, except this fellow's a south-paw." If he wins, you say, "I told you he reminded me of Al Brown," and if he loses, "Well, well, I guess he's no Al Brown. They don't make fighters like Al any more." This identifies you as a man who (a) has been in Paris, (b) has been going to fights for a long time, and (c) therefore enjoys what the fellows who write for quarterlies call a frame of reference.

It may be argued that this doesn't get you anywhere, but it at least constitutes what a man I once met named Thomas S. Matthews called communication. Mr. Matthews, who was the editor of *Time*, said that the most important thing in journalism is not reporting but communication. "What are you going to communicate?" I asked him. "The most important thing," he said, "is the man on one end of the circuit saying 'My God, I'm alive! You're alive!' and the fellow on the other end, receiving his message, saying 'My God, you're right! We're both alive!'" I still think it is a hell of a way to run a news magazine, but it is a good reason for going to fights in person. Television, if unchecked, may carry us back to a pre-tribal state of social development, when the family was the largest conversational unit.

Fights are also a great place for adding to your repertory of witty sayings. I shall not forget my adolescent delight when I first heard a fight fan yell, "I hope youse bot' gets knocked out!" I thought he had made it up, although I found out later it was a cliché. It is a formula adaptable to an endless variety of situations outside the ring. The only trouble with it is it never works out. The place where I first heard the line was Bill Brown's, a fight club in a big shed behind a trolley station in Far Rockaway.

On another night there, the time for the main bout arrived and one of the principals hadn't. The other fighter sat in the ring, a bantamweight with a face like a well-worn coin, and the fans stamped in cadence and whistled and yelled for their money back. It was thirty years before television, but there were only a couple of hundred men on hand. The preliminary fights had been terrible. The little fighter kept looking at his hands, which were resting on his knees in cracked boxing gloves, and every now and then he would spit on the mat and rub the spittle into the canvas with one of his scuffed ring shoes. The longer he waited, the more frequently he spat, and I presumed he was worrying about the money he was supposed to get; it wouldn't be more than fifty dollars with a house that size, even if the other man turned up. He had come there from some remote place like West or East New York, and he may have been thinking about the last train home on the Long Island Railroad, too. Finally, the other bantamweight got there, looking out of breath and flustered. He had lost his way on the railroad—changed to the wrong train at Jamaica and had to go back there and start over. The crowd booed so loud that he looked embarrassed. When the fight began, the fellow who had been waiting walked right into the new boy and knocked him down. He acted impatient. The tardy fellow got up and fought back gamely, but the one who had been waiting nailed him again, and the latecomer just about pulled up to one knee at the count of seven. He had been hit pretty hard, and you could see from his face that he was wondering whether to chuck it. Somebody in the crowd yelled out, "Hey, Hickey! You kept us all waiting! Why don't you stay around awhile?" So the fellow got up and caught for ten rounds and probably made the one who had come early miss his train. It's another formula with multiple applications, and I think the man who said it that night in Far Rockaway did make it up.

Because of the way I feel about watching fights on television, I was highly pleased when I read, back in June, 1951, that the fifteen-round match between Joe Louis and Lee Savold, scheduled for June thirteenth at the Polo Grounds, was to be neither televised, except to eight theater audiences in places like Pittsburgh and Albany, nor broadcast over the radio. I hadn't seen Louis with the naked eye since we shook hands in a pub in London in 1944. He had fought often since then, and I had seen his two bouts with Jersey Joe Walcott on television, but there hadn't been any fun in it. Those had been held in public places, naturally, and I could have gone, but television gives you so plausible an adumbration of a fight, for nothing, that you feel it would be extravagant to pay your way in. It is like the potato, which is only a succedaneum for something decent to eat but which, once introduced into Ireland, proved so cheap that the peasants gave up their grain-and-meat diet in favor of it. After that, the landlords let them keep just enough money to buy potatoes. William Cobbett, a great Englishman, said that he would sack any workmen of his he caught eating one of the cursed things, because as soon as potatoes appeared anywhere they brought down the standard of eating. I sometimes think of Cobbett on my way home from the races, looking at the television aerials on all the little houses between here and Belmont Park. As soon as I heard that the fight wouldn't be on the air, I determined to buy a ticket.

On the night of the thirteenth, a Wednesday, it rained, and

on the next night it rained again, so on the evening of June fifteenth the promoters, the International Boxing Club, confronted by a night game at the Polo Grounds, transferred the fight to Madison Square Garden. The postponements upset a plan I had had to go to the fight with a friend, who had another date for the third night. But alone is a good way to go to a fight or the races, because you have more time to look around you, and you always get all the conversation you can use anyway. I went to the Garden box office early Friday afternoon and bought a ten-dollar seat in the side arena—the first tiers rising in back of the boxes, midway between Eighth and Ninth Avenues on the 49th Street side of the house. There was only a scattering of ticket buyers in the lobby, and the man at the ticket window was polite—a bad omen for the gate. After buying the ticket, I got into a cab in front of the Garden, and the driver naturally asked me if I was going to see the fight. I said I was, and he said, "He's all through."

I knew he meant Louis, and I said, "I know, and that's why it may be a good fight. If he weren't through, he might kill this guy."

The driver said, "Savold is a hooker. He breaks noses."

I said, "He couldn't break his own nose, even," and then began to wonder how a man would go about trying to do that. "It's a shame he's so hard up he had to fight at all at his age," I said, knowing the driver would understand I meant Louis. I was surprised that the driver was against Louis, and I was appealing to his better feelings.

"He must have plenty socked away," said the driver. "Playing golf for a hundred dollars a hole."

"Maybe that helped him go broke," I said. "And anyway, what does that prove? There's many a man with a small salary who bets more than he can afford." I had seen a scratch sheet on the seat next to the hackie. I was glad I was riding only as far as Brentano's with him.

The driver I had on the long ride home was a better type. As soon as I told him I was going to the fight, which was at about the same time that he dropped the flag, he said, "I guess the old guy can still sock."

I said, "I saw him murder Max Baer sixteen years ago. He was a sweet fighter then."

The driver said, "Sixteen years is a long time for a fighter. I don't remember anybody lasted sixteen years in the big money. Still, Savold is almost as old as he is. When you're a bum, nobody notices how old you get."

We had a pleasant time on the West Side Highway, talking about how Harry Greb had gone on fighting when he was blind in one eye, only nobody knew it but his manager, and how Pete Herman had been the best in-fighter in the world, because he had been practically blind in both eyes, so he couldn't afford to fool around outside. "What Herman did, you couldn't learn a boy now," the driver said. "They got no patience."

The fellow who drove me from my house to the Garden after dinner was also a man of good will, but rather different. He knew I was going to the fight as soon as I told him my destination, and once we had got under way, he said, "It is a pity that a man like Louis should be exploited to such a degree that he has to fight again." It was only nine-fifteen, and he agreed with me that I had plenty of time to get to the Garden for the main bout, which was scheduled to begin at ten, but when we got caught in unexpectedly heavy traffic on Eleventh Avenue he grew impatient. "Come on, Jersey!" he said, giving a station wagon in front of us the horn. "In the last analysis, we have got to get to the Garden sometime." But it didn't help much, because most of the other cars were heading for the Garden, too. The traffic was so slow going toward Eighth Avenue on Fiftieth Street that I asked him to let me out near the Garden corner, and joined the people hurrying from the Independent Subway exit toward the Garden marquee. A high percentage of them were from Harlem, and they were dressed as if for a levee, the men in shimmering gabardines and felt hats the color of freshly unwrapped chewing gum, the women in spring suits and fur pieces—it was a cool night—and what seemed to me the prettiest hats of the season. They seemed to me the prettiest lot of women I had seen in a long time, too, and I reflected that if the fight had been televised, I would have missed them. "Step out," I heard one beau say as his group swept past me, "or we won't maybe get in. It's just like I told you—he's still one hell of a draw." As I made my way through the now crowded lobby, I could hear the special cop next to the ticket window chanting, "Six-, eight-, ten-, and fifteen-dollar tickets only," which meant that the two-and-a-half-dollar general-admission and the twenty-dollar ringside seats were sold out. It made me feel good, because it showed there were still some gregarious people left in the world.

Inside the Garden there was the same old happy drone of voices as when Jimmy McLarnin was fighting and Jimmy Walker was at the ringside. There was only one small patch of bare seats, in a particularly bad part of the ringside section. I wondered what sort of occupant I would find in my seat; I knew from experience that there would be somebody in it. It turned out to be a small, frail colored man in wine-red livery. He sat up straight and pressed his shoulder blades against the back of the chair, so I couldn't see the number. When I showed him my ticket, he said, "I don't know nothing about that. You better see the usher." He was offering this token resistance, I knew, only to protect his self-esteem—to maintain the shadowy fiction that he was in the seat by error. When an usher wandered within hailing distance of us, I called him, and the little man left, to drift to some other part of the Garden, where he had no reputation as a ten-dollar-seat holder to lose, and there to squat contentedly on a step.

My seat was midway between the east and west ends of the ring, and about fifteen feet above it. Two not very skillful colored boys were finishing a four-rounder that the man in the next seat told me was an emergency bout, put on because there had been several knockouts in the earlier preliminaries. It gave me a chance to settle down and look around. It was ten o'clock by the time the colored boys finished and the man with the microphone announced the decision, but there was no sign of Louis or Savold. The fight wasn't on the air, so there was no need of the punctuality required by the radio business. (Later I read in the newspapers that the bout had been delayed in deference to the hundreds of people who were still in line to buy tickets and who wanted to be sure of seeing the whole fight.) Nobody made any spiel about beer, as on the home screen, although a good volume of it was being drunk all around. Miss Gladys Gooding, an organist, played the national anthem and a tenor sang it, and we all applauded. After that, the announcer introduced a number of less than illustrious prizefighters from the ring, but nobody whistled or acted restless. It was a good-natured crowd.

Then Louis and his seconds—what the author of *Boxiana* would have called his faction—appeared from a runway under the north stands and headed toward the ring. The first thing I noticed, from where I sat, was that the top of Louis's head was bald. He looked taller than I had remembered him, although surely he couldn't have grown after the age of thirty, and his face was puffy and impassive. It has always been so. In the days of his greatness, the press read menace in it. He walked stifflegged, as was natural for a heavy man of thirty-seven, but when his seconds pulled off his dressing robe, his body looked all right. He had never been a lean man; his muscles had always been well buried beneath his smooth beige skin. I recalled the first time I had seen him fight—against Baer. That was at the Yankee Stadium, in September, 1935, and not only the great ball park but the roofs of all the apartment houses around were crowded with spectators, and hundreds of people were getting out of trains at the elevated I.R.T. station, which overlooks the field, and trying to loiter long enough to catch a few moments of action. Louis had come East that summer, after a single year as a professional, and had knocked out Primo Carnera in a few rounds. Carnera had been the heavyweight champion of the world in 1934, when Baer knocked him out. Baer, when he fought Louis, was the most powerful and gifted heavyweight of the day, although he had already fumbled away his title. But this mature Baer, who had fought everybody, was frightened stiff by the twenty-one-year-old mulatto boy. Louis outclassed him. The whole thing went only four rounds. There hadn't been anybody remotely like Louis since Dempsey in the early twenties.

The week of the Louis-Baer fight, a man I know wrote in a magazine: "With half an eye, one can observe that the town is more full of stir than it has been in many moons. It is hard to find a place to park, hard to get a table in a restaurant, hard to answer all the phone calls. . . . Economic seers can explain it, if you care to listen. We prefer to remember that a sudden inflation of the town's spirit can be just as much psychological or accidental as economic." I figured it was Louis.

Savold had now come up into the other corner, a jutty-jawed man with a fair skin but a red back, probably sunburned at his training camp. He was twenty pounds lighter than Louis, but that isn't considered a crushing handicap among heavy-weights; Ezzard Charles, who beat Louis the previous year, was ten pounds lighter than Savold. Savold was thirty-five, and there didn't seem to be much bounce in him. I had seen him fight twice in the winter of 1946, and I knew he wasn't much. Both bouts had been against a young Negro heavyweight named Al Hoosman, a tall, skinny fellow just out of the Army. Hoosman had started well the first time, but Savold had hurt him with body punches and won the decision. The second time, Hoosman had stayed away and jabbed him silly. An old third-rater like Savold, I knew, doesn't improve with five more years on him. But an old third-rater doesn't rattle easily, either, and I was sure he'd do his best. It made me more apprehensive, in one way, than if he'd been any good. I wouldn't have liked to see Louis beaten by a good young fighter, but it would be awful to see him beaten by a clown. Not that I have any-thing against Savold; I just think it's immoral for a fellow with-out talent to get too far. A lot of others in the crowd must have felt the same way, because the house was quiet when the fight started—as if the Louis rooters didn't want to ask too much of Joe. There weren't any audible rooters for Savold, though, of course, there would have been if he had landed one good punch.

I remembered reading in a newspaper that Savold had said he would walk right out and bang Louis in the temple with a right, which would scramble his thinking. But all he did was come forward as he had against Hoosman, with his left low. A fellow like that never changes. Louis walked out straight and stiff-legged, and jabbed his left into Savold's face. He did it again and again, and Savold didn't seem to know what to do about it. And Louis jabs a lot harder than a fellow like Hoos-man. Louis didn't have to chase Savold, and he had no reason to run away from him, either, so the stiff legs were all right. When the two men came close together, Louis jarred Savold with short punches, and Savold couldn't push him around, so that was all right, too. After the first round, the crowd knew Louis would win if his legs would hold him.

In the second round Louis began hitting Savold with combinations—quick sequences of punches, like a right under the heart and a left hook to the right side of the head. A sports writer I know had told me that Louis hadn't been putting combinations together for several fights back. Combinations demand a superior kind of coordination, but a fighter who has once had that can partly regain it by hard work. A couple of times it looked as if Louis was trying for a knockout, but when Savold didn't come apart, Louis returned to jabbing. A man somewhere behind me kept saying to a companion, "I read Savold was a tricky fighter. He's got to do something!" But Savold didn't, until late in the fifth round, by which time his head must have felt like a sick music box. Then he threw a right to Louis's head and it landed. I thought I could see Louis shrink, as if he feared trouble. His response ten years ago would have been to tear right back into the man. Savold threw another right, exactly the same kind, and that hit Louis, too. No good fighter should have been hit twice in succession with that kind of foolish punch. But the punches weren't hard enough to slow Louis down, and that was the end of that. In the third minute of the sixth round, he hit Savold with a couple of combinations no harder than those that had gone before, but Savold was weak now. His legs were going limp, and Louis was pursuing him as he backed toward my side of the ring. Then Louis swung like an axman with his right (he wasn't snapping it as he used to), and his left dropped over Savold's guard and against his jaw, and the fellow was rolling over and over on the mat, rolling the way football players do when they fall on a fumbled ball. The referee was counting and Savold was rolling, and he got up on either nine or ten, I couldn't tell which (later, I read that it was ten, so he was out officially), but you could see he was knocked silly, and the referee had his arms around him, and it was over.

The newspapermen, acres of them near the ring, were banging out the leads for the running stories they had already telegraphed, and I felt sorry for them, because they never have time to enjoy boxing matches. Since the fight was not broadcast, there was no oily-voiced chap to drag Louis over to a microphone and ask him stupid questions. He shook hands with Savold twice, once right after the knockout and again a few minutes later, when Savold was ready to leave the ring, as if he feared Savold wouldn't remember the first handshake.

I drifted toward the lobby with the crowd. The chic Harlem people were saying to one another, "It was terrific, darling! It was terrific!" I could see that an element of continuity had been restored to their world. But there wasn't any of the wild exultation that had followed those first Louis victories in 1935. These people had celebrated so many times—except, of course, the younger ones, who were small children when Louis knocked out Baer. I recognized one of the Garden promoters, usually a sour fellow, looking happy. The bout had brought in receipts of $94,684, including my ten dollars, but, what was more important to the Garden, Louis was sure to draw a lot more the next time, and at a higher scale of prices.

I walked downtown on Eighth Avenue to a point where the crowd began to thin out, and climbed into a taxi that had been stopped by the light on a cross street. This one had a Negro driver.

"The old fellow looked pretty good tonight," I said. "Had those combinations going."

"Fight over?" the driver asked. If there had been television, or even radio, he would have known about everything, and I wouldn't have had the fun of telling him.

"Sure," I said. "He knocked the guy out in the sixth."

"I was afraid he wouldn't," said the driver. "You know, it's a funny thing," he said, after we had gone on a way, "but I been twenty-five years in New York now and never seen Joe Louis in the flesh."

"You've seen him on television, haven't you?"

"Yeah," he said. "But that don't count." After a while he said, "I remember when he fought Carnera. The celebration in Harlem. They poisoned his mind before that fight, his managers and Jack Blackburn did. They told him Carnera was Mussolini's man and Mussolini started the Ethiopian War. He cut that man down like he was a tree."

BROKEN FIGHTER ARRIVES

WHEN Louis knocked Savold out, I came away singularly revived—as if I, rather than Louis, had demonstrated resistance to the erosion of time. As long as Joe could get by, I felt, I had a link with an era when we were both a lot younger. Only the great champions give their fellow citizens time to feel that way about them, because only the great ones win the title young and hold on to it. There have been three like that among the heavyweights in this century—Jim Jeffries, Jack Dempsey, and Louis. Jeffries won the championship in 1899, when my father was a foot-loose young sport, and was beaten, after a period of retirement, by Jack Johnson in 1910, when Father was a solemn burgher with a wife, two children, and three twelve-story loft buildings with second mortgages on them. Dempsey beat Jess Willard in 1919, when I was in short pants. He lost the second decision to Gene Tunney in 1927 (I had believed that the first was an accident, and so I had continued to think of him as champion), and by that time I had written half a novel, spent a year at the Sorbonne, and worked on two newspapers.

Louis was the champion, in the public mind, from 1935, when he slaughtered Primo Carnera and Max Baer, until 1951. Technically, his span was slightly shorter, because he didn't beat Jim Braddock for the title until 1937, but everybody knew from 1935 on that he would beat Braddock whenever he got the match. And he lost the championship by a decision to Ezzard Charles in 1950, but Charles was subsequently knocked out by old Jersey Joe Walcott, whom Louis had flattened a while back. When the three were introduced from the ring before the bout between Sugar Ray Robinson and Randy Turpin in September, 1951, the crowd left no doubt that it still considered Louis the leading heavyweight.

At about that same time, I learned that Louis, who was thirty-seven, had been "made" with a new heavyweight, Rocky Marciano, who was twenty-seven and a puncher. I didn't think much about it then, but as October twenty-sixth, the date set for the fight, approached, I began to feel uneasy. Marciano, to be sure, had never had a professional fight until shortly after Louis first announced his retirement, in 1948. (Joe had subsequently, of course, recanted.) In addition, Marciano had beaten only two opponents of any note, both young heavyweights like himself, who were rated as no better than promising. He was not big for a heavyweight, and was supposed to be rather crude. What bothered me, though, about the impending affair was that Marciano was, as he still is, steered by a man I know, named Al Weill, who is one of the most realistic fellows in a milieu where illusions are few. Marciano was already a good drawing card and would continue to be as long as he was unbeaten, and Weill, I was sure, would never risk the depreciation of an asset unless he felt he had a good bet.

Weill is at present the matchmaker of the I.B.C., which controls boxing here in New York and in a dozen other large cities, and his son, Marty Weill, is Marciano's manager "of record," which means he signs the contracts. The younger Weill has a job-lot commission business in Dayton, Ohio, and isn't properly a boxing man at all. When the elder Weill became matchmaker, he "gave" his son the fighter, much as a lawyer, upon becoming a public official, turns over his private practice to a partner. Marciano is, in effect, a kind of family enterprise, like Rockefeller Center. As the fight date drew near, I decided to go around to the headquarters of the International, above the Iceland Skating Rink in the Madison Square Garden building, and ask the elder Weill what was doing. I could have accomplished this less formally by giving him what he calls a bang on the telephone, but I wished to compare his facial expressions with his asseverations.

The matchmaker is of the build referred to in ready-made-clothing stores as a portly, which means not quite a stout. There is an implication of at least one kind of recklessness about a fat man; he lets himself go when he eats. A portly man, on the other hand, is a man who would like to be fat but restrains himself—a calculator. Weill has a Roman nose of the short, or budgereegah, variety, and an over-all grayish coloration that is complemented by the suits he generally wears and the cigar ashes he frequently spills on them. On his home block—86th Street between West End Avenue and Riverside Drive—he blends perfectly with the tired 1910 grandeur of the apartment houses; he looks like one more garment manufacturer worried by a swollen inventory. This does not stop him from knowing more about the fight business than any of the flashier types who wear long beige jackets and stay downtown after dark.

Weill is a frugal man, and he likes frugal fighters. Every kind of serious trouble a fighter can get into, he says, has its origin in the disbursement of currency—rich food, liquor, women, horse-race betting, and fast automobiles. Once a fighter starts gambling, Weill doesn't want him. "A gambler thinks he can get money without working for it," he says. Weill had a big string of fighters before the war, and used to quarter them all in a lodging house near Central Park West, where the house-master would issue to each boy a weekly meal ticket with a face value of five dollars and fifty cents, redeemable in trade at a coffeepot on Columbus Avenue. The tickets cost Weill five dollars each, cash. A fighter could get a second ticket before the week was out, but only if he showed that the first one had been punched out to the last nickel. None of those fighters ever suffered a defeat that could be attributed to high living. Mere frugality, however, may prove a boomerang, for the fighter sometimes gets to like it. There was once an old colored heavyweight named Bob Armstrong, who, when asked his utmost ambition, said, "To wake up every morning and find a dollar under my pillow." Naturally, he never got to be champion. Weill wouldn't want a fighter like that. What he really loves is an avaricious fighter.

When I asked Weill about Marciano he looked happy. "He is a nice boy," he said. "The dollar is his God. That is to say, he is a poor Italian boy from a large, poor family, and he appreciates the buck more than almost anybody else. Them type guys is hard to get outa there. You want to look out for them young broken fighters." By "broken fighter," Weill, who is a purist, meant a fighter who is broke. "He only got two hallway decent purses—with LaStarza and Layne—and it was like a tiger tasting blood," Weill went on. "So you know how confident he is when he will take a fight like this for fifteen per cent of the gate. Louis gets forty-five. Why, Marciano will bring more money into the Garden than Louis. Connecticut, Rhode Island, and half of Massachusetts will be empty that night." Marciano hails from Brockton, Massachusetts.

Having considered the morale factor, which with him always comes first, Weill passed to the tactical level. He said Marciano would never be a clever boxer; he wasn't made for it, anyway, being short for a heavyweight, and wide, with short, thick arms. "But he knows what he has to do," Weill said. "Get in close enough to hit and then keep on hitting. And he don't come walking in straight, like Savold. Anybody would look good punching a punching bag that comes straight to you. This kid will fight out of a crouch. How I got him"—he changed the subject abruptly—"is three years ago a fellow I know used to promote around Boston wrote me there was a hell of an amateur he would like me to take. So I sent up the carfare for them to come down. They come, and we took Rocky to the C.Y.O. gym and put him in with a young heavyweight from Staten Island, a big blond guy belonged to a friend of mine. We had to stop him or he'd killed that Staten Island guy. I seen right then Rocky had the beginning of it. So I sent him up to Manny Almeida, a friend of mine promotes in Providence, which is near where he is out of Brockton, but Brockton is too small to have fights. And I asked Manny to put him in with the same kind he was, but no setups. Because you got a guy knocking over setups, you don't know what you got. He come along good. When I come over here, I give him to Marty. Who should I give him to if not my own flesh and blood?"

A day or two after my talk with Weill, I went out to Louis's training quarters at Pompton Lakes, New Jersey, and it was like going back to the first administration of Franklin D. Roosevelt. There was about all Louis's habits a majestic continuity, as there was about his style in the ring, which is basically classical. His style has diminished in speed of execution but has never varied in concept. Pompton was his lucky camp; he trained there for his first New York fight, against Carnera, in 1935, when he was twenty-one, and he trained there for all his succeeding fights but four—"way more than twenty," he told me when I talked with him later that day. I hadn't been out there since the summer of 1938, when Louis was preparing for his return fight with Max Schmeling, the only man who had up to that time knocked him out. (That return fight was his happiest victory; he destroyed the German in less than a round.) Incidentally, Louis has knocked out six men who at one time or another held the heavyweight championship—Schmeling, Jack

Sharkey, Carnera, Baer, Braddock, and Walcott—a record possible because the championship changed hands so often in the short period between 1930 and 1937, leaving so many mediocre ex-champions simultaneously extant.

The camp, like Louis himself, was essentially the same but much older-looking. Part of the difference, I suppose, was due to the fact that the Schmeling fight had been in the summer, and now the leaves were turning on the sides of the Ramapos, and the air was chill. But that wasn't all of it. Before the war, the camp was operated by a bright and energetic couple named Dr. and Mrs. Bier, who had ambitions about turning it into a health farm for millionaires. On days when Louis was to spar, the grounds were always packed with charabancs from Harlem bringing people to see him work. The money pouring in at the gate, at a dollar a head, made training actually a profitable activity, and the hot-dog concession alone—there was also a bar—brought in enough to pay the sparring partners. The place has since been bought by a man by the name of Baumgartner, and there is no longer a bar, or even a hot dog, on the premises, although I heard that Coca-Cola can be bought on Sundays. The day I was there, there were perhaps a dozen automobiles on the grounds when sparring was scheduled to begin, and no more than twenty-five paying customers, at sixty cents a head, despite the fact that the fight was only a week off. And, except for me, the press was represented only by Colonel John R. Stingo, who writes a column called "Yea Verily" for the New York *Enquirer*, a newspaper always dated Monday but published only on Sunday afternoon. Colonel Stingo is a small, agile man who helped cover the Corbett-Sullivan fight for the New Orleans *Item* in 1892. A Boston newspaperman named Gilhooley had ridden out with us from New York in a car hired by the I.B.C., but had gone on to Marciano's training camp at Greenwood Lake, New York, seventeen miles farther along. The car was to wait there for him, and then pick us up after the workouts were over.

One of the first things I saw on getting out of the car was a familiar sweatered figure sprawled in a lawn chair in front of the red frame building that in livelier days housed the bar. It was Mannie Seamon, Louis's trainer, a white man who stepped into the job after the death of Jack Blackburn, the old colored

fighter who formed Louis's style. Seamon is more of a condi-
tioner than a boxing coach—a jovial, rosy-cheeked man who
sometimes discourses learnedly on "bone juice" and keeping
the air out of his charges' bones. He hadn't changed at all in the
intervening years, I noted enviously, but I winced when I
thought of how many thousand medicine balls he must have
thrown at Louis's and other fighters' stomachs since 1938.
All the sparring partners of thirteen years ago were gone—
working on the docks, most of them, Seamon said—and so
were Louis's managers then, John Roxborough and Julian
Black, the two colored sporting men who brought Joe out of
the Middle West, and Mike Jacobs, the quondam ticket scalper
who once controlled boxing through his control of that great
new favorite, Louis.

"Joe's looking the best he has in four years," Mannie said.
(It was in 1947, in his first match against Walcott, that Louis
first showed he was slipping badly.) We talked a while about
fellows we had known in the thirties, and I asked Mannie if the
terrible monotony of training wasn't beginning to tell on
Louis. Joe made his pro debut in 1934, and he had boxed amateur before that, and the Army meant no letup, for his duty
there consisted of boxing exhibitions for other soldiers. So he
had been at it for nearly twenty years—light bag, heavy bag,
pushups, belly bends, roadwork, and shadowboxing. It is hard
to stay interested in your own shadow for twenty years. Even
an old race horse gets so he won't extend himself in works.

"We keep his mind off it as much as we can," Seamon said.
"We got a rule here, we never talk fight. Anything but that. We
listen to phonograph records, or we play cards, or handicap
horses. I tell him funny stories, and the best is different people
come in and talk to him."

Seamon walked over to the gymnasium to get the fighter
ready for his sparring exhibition, and after a while Colonel
Stingo and I followed him. When we got to the dressing
room, Louis was sitting on the rubbing table while Seamon
prepared his hands—bandages, gauze, and flat sponge-rubber
pads over the knuckles, and then adhesive tape to hold the
structure in place. Seamon said, "Joe, this is Colonel Stingo.
He is seventy-eight years old and he wants to work a couple of
rounds with you." Louis looked down at the Colonel and

couldn't at the moment think of anything to say except "Glad to meet you." I reminded Louis that he and I had last met in Frisco's, a drinking club on Sackville Street, in London, during the war, and he said, "That man once charged me sixteen dollars for a pint of gin." With us in the dressing room was a slender colored man named Reed, a friend of Louis's who had evidently been a patron of Frisco's at the same time, and he joined in the conversation to say he had once paid a cabby three pounds and six shillings to drive him to Frisco's from a few streets away. " 'Three-and-six,' the man said," Reed recalled. "So I gave him three pounds and six shillings, and then I reached in my pocket and all I had left was a ten-shilling note, so I gave it to him for a tip. I didn't know if it was enough. That was my first time on leave in London." Louis began to laugh. "That was a pretty good tip," he said. "Two dollars for a seventy-cent ride that you already paid him nearly fifteen bucks for."

Louis, Reed, and I began telling stories about prices we had paid in London, straining the elastic of credulity with each tale—a kind of auction. Louis stuck closest to plausibility; Reed and I were just trying to be funny. Fruit had been fantastically dear in London by American standards, and Louis said he had once paid thirty shillings for a pound of hothouse grapes, as a present for an English family he knew. "Then I saw just a small apple there for six shillings," he said. "So I bought that, and bit into it outside the store. Man, it was sour! I give the rest of it to an old dog that come along, and he took one bite and took off." Louis also told about going up on a roof to watch an air raid his first night in London. "The tracers was the most beautiful thing I ever saw," he said.

By the time Seamon had finished with his hands, Louis was in high good humor. "I'm sorry we got no boxing shoes to fit you, Colonel," he said to Stingo just before he went into the gymnasium. "So I guess I won't be able to work with you today. You worked with me wearing those shoes, you might step all over my feet and disable me."

There was nothing showy about the workout. Two of Louis's three partners were light heavyweights, much smaller than the old champion, and they worked fast, to speed up his reflexes. He didn't punch hard at either, since the idea wasn't to discourage them. One of them, a brown boy from Bermuda, hit Louis pretty freely, but it was reasonable to suppose the Bermudian was a lot faster than Marciano could possibly be. That's the point of working with a light, fast man. The only partner on hand of the big, rough type that used to staff Louis's camps was a heavyweight named Elkins Brothers, whom I had seen fight in the semifinal on the Robinson-Turpin card. Brothers, a squat, powerful fellow, played the part of Marciano when he sparred with Louis. He came in crouching, and threw overhand rights at Louis's jaw. The overhand right, thrown in a rising arc like an artillery shell, was supposed to be Marciano's best punch. Louis kept jabbing at Brothers' head, trying to hit him just as the right started coming and keep him off balance. When he succeeded, he stepped in with a right uppercut. It was a pattern of battle, but neither man pressed it to its ultimate implication. They were methodical rather than fierce. Louis's body looked good—leaner, if anything, than it had in 1938—and the jab was as sweet as ever.

Stingo and I were sitting out on the lawn after the workout, waiting for the car from Greenwood Lake to pick us up, when Louis came along, on his way from the gym to his living quarters. He looked younger with his snap-brim hat on. It hid the bald spot. And in street clothes, after all, a superbly conditioned man of thirty-seven is still young. It's when he gets into a ring that age comes on him. Louis hovered over us for a while, but none of us could think of much to say. It was no use asking him how he felt, or whether he thought he could win this one, because clearly he was as good as anybody could get him now, and he had never had a match in his life that he didn't think he was going to win, and sixty-nine times out of seventy-one he had been right. So why would he change his mind this time?

Louis gave a small shiver and said, "Well, I guess I better go in, or I might get a chill." We shook hands all around, and he went along to play cards with the sparring partners who belonged to a younger generation.

The camp at Greenwood Lake, which I visited three days before the fight, was more lively. Marciano looked like the

understander in the nine-man pyramid of a troupe of Arab acrobats. He was bull-necked and wide-shouldered, and even
when he was merely walking around in the ring, he kept rip-
pling the muscles of his arms and back, as if afraid that if he
let them set they would tie up. He looks as if he should be
muscle-bound, but he isn't. He worked with a big, rangy young
heavyweight named Jimmy DeLange, who had the Louis role,
and they fought as if they wanted to transcend the limitations
of the leather head guards and the huge sparring gloves and
knock each other out. Marciano moved around briskly on his
stubby legs and threw punches well, especially to the body, but
DeLange had no trouble reaching his head with left jabs, and
the spar-mate's right uppercuts to the body came off well in
close. Marciano was working in a head guard that was a cross
between a gladiatorial helmet and race-horse blinkers, with
long leather wings at the sides of his eyes. He wouldn't have
that, at any rate, when he fought Louis, I told myself. He finished the third, and last, round with a big burst of punching.

During the workout, I sat alongside the ancient featherweight champion Abe Attell, and after it was over and the
trainers had pulled Marciano's gloves off, Abe called up to the
fighter, "Take it easy, Rocky! He's only a sparring partner!"
The fighter held up three fingers and called back apologeti-
cally, "Only tree days!"—signifying that, with but three days
to go, he was in too good shape to restrain himself.

"I had five hundred on him," Attell said to me. "And after
what I seen today I'm making it a thousand." Attell, who was
himself one of the greatest of boxers, is a knowing man about
fights, but he is famous for having an intricate mind. I con-
soled myself with the thought that he might, in fact, be betting on Louis and speaking favorably of Marciano only to get
the odds up.

"Louis is all through," Attell went on, with what I considered a deplorable lack of sentiment in an old champion who
had himself felt the sharp tooth of time. But Attell, who looks
at you with cold eyes around his huge beak that is like a tou-
can's with a twisted septum, is not a sentimental man. "If they
get a referee who don't let Louis hang on, the kid will knock
him out," he said. He then put a handful of BB shot in his
mouth and started to pick his teeth. He uses bamboo tooth-

picks, which he has tailored for him at a novelty shop on Broadway. From time to time, by means of his toothpick, he propels the pellets, one by one, through gaps between his teeth, hitting with perfect accuracy any object up to ten feet away. A night-club hostess with a plunging neckline is his favorite target, but a busy bartender in a dimly lighted joint will keep him almost equally happy. *En villégiature*, he will take targets of opportunity, like the back of a stranger's neck. "I got hit with an automobile a couple years ago and got three new choppers on the right side, with no holes between then," he told me. "So now I developed a curve out the left."

Leaving the unfeeling Mr. Attell, I went over to wait outside the dressing room for Charlie Goldman, Marciano's trainer, an old bantamweight who has coached Weill's fighters for years. Goldman is a fine pedagogue, because he brings out his pupil's qualities instead of trying to change them. "The great thing about this kid is he's got leverage," he told me when he came out of the dressing room. "He takes a good punch and he's got the equalizers. He had leverage from the start, and when you teach a fellow like that, you have to go slow, because you might change the way he stands or the way he moves, and spoil his hitting. Everything new you show him, you have to ask him, 'Does it feel natural?' 'Can you hit from there?' So naturally he'll never be a flashy boxer. But he's in the improving phase. He's still six months—maybe a year—away. But whether he beats Louis or not, he's going to be a lot better next summer."

Goldman is a soft-spoken, merry little man with a large head, buffed to a plane surface in front, and a pair of hands that look as if they had been trampled on. "Looka the bum, how many times he broke his hands!" Attell says loftily. His own magnificent fists carried him through three hundred and sixty-five fights with only one break. Goldman's more friable maulies prevented him from knocking out many of the four hundred opponents he fought, but they made him a thoughtful kind of boxer.

"Most fighters at twenty-seven have been boxing eight, nine years, and they are as good as they ever will be," Goldman told me. "But Rocky has only had about the equivalent of one year's experience. So he's still learning. Every time we made a fight for him up in New England, we would bring him down to New York for a week and get him a room at the C.Y.O., and then he would work out four or five afternoons at Stillman's," he said. "But he didn't do as much boxing in the three years as one of the boys who's at Stillman's every day would do in a year. So he's just beginning to come along. He'll knock them all out."

When I entered Madison Square Garden on the night of the fight I couldn't help hoping that Marciano was still too far away to demolish Louis. His day was bound to come anyway, if Goldman was right, and I wanted to see Louis get by once more. My seat was about where I had sat when I watched Louis beat Savold. I was sitting well forward in the mezzanine on the 49th Street side, midway between the east and west ends of the ring, at a point where I could watch crowd as well as fighters.

There were the usual introductions from the ring of white and colored men in knee-length jackets with flaring shoulders —rough, tough Paddy DeMarco, Philadelphia's undefeated Gil Turner, Sugar Ray Robinson, former heavyweight champion Ezzard Charles, and, finally, Jersey Joe Walcott, the reigning champion, as old as Louis by his own statement, several years older by popular report. ("I'm not old," he told a sports writer in 1947. "I'm just ugly.") The names of the judges and referee were announced: Joe Agnello, Harold Barnes, Ruby Goldstein —no surprises. And then the two factions were in the ring— Louis's in the northwest corner, Marciano's in the southeast. Mannie Seamon and a couple of fellows I didn't know were with Louis; Goldman and Marty Weill were with Marciano, together with a fellow New Englander named Al Columbo. Weill, a thin, pale young man with rumpled hair, seemed more awed than his fighter. Marciano was bouncing on his thick legs and punching the air to warm up. A tall, ash-blond woman near me was saying, "I hate him! I hate him! I think he's the most horrible thing I've ever seen." This struck me as being hard on Rocky; he didn't look particularly repulsive. Husky as he was, he looked slight compared to Louis, who was three inches taller and, according to the announced weights, twenty-five pounds heavier. When the fighters were introduced, it was evident that if Connecticut, Rhode Island, and half of Massachusetts were not completely empty, their populations were at least substantially depleted for the evening. The Marciano supporters were cheering him as if he were a high-school football team. But Louis got an even bigger welcome.

And then, as the immortal historian of the British ring, Pierce Egan, wrote of the third fight between Dan Mendoza and Dick Humphries, in 1789, "The awful set-to at length commenced—when every eye beamed with anxiety—the moment was interesting and attractive, and each party was lost in suspense." I had a pair of pocket binoculars, 6 × 15s, and I kept them trained on Louis for the first half minute. His face was impassive, as usual, but his actions showed that he wasn't taking the strong boy lightly. Instead of moving relentlessly forward, as in his great days, he seemed to be waiting to see what he was up against. In the first clinches, it was he who shifted Marciano, and not the other way about; Louis was stronger than the strong boy—at the beginning, anyway. He could outbox him at a distance, and if he could continue to smother him in close, I thought he would get by. Up to the last five seconds of the round, I noted, glancing at the ringside clock, neither of them had done anything remarkable, and that was all right with me. I had had a feeling that Marciano might rush out of his corner throwing punches and try to take Louis by storm. Then Marciano threw one of those rights, and it landed, it seemed to me, just under Louis's left ear. Louis had dropped his left shoulder after jabbing—an old fault, which brought about most of the bad moments of his career. This was the kind of punch that addles a man's brains, and if it had happened thirty seconds earlier and Marciano had pressed his advantage, he might have knocked Louis out in the first round.

I think that punch was the one that made Joe feel old. Between the rounds, I could see Seamon pressing an ice bag against the back of Louis's neck, and when I turned my binoculars on Charlie Goldman's face, he was grinning. Louis was apparently clearheaded when he came out for the second, but he didn't do much. I thought he won the next three rounds, jabbing Marciano's face and jolting him with rights in close. But the rights didn't sicken Marciano, as they had sickened Louis's opponents from 1935 to 1940; he reacted as if he were being hit by just an ordinary fighter. Marciano was missing almost all his own swings, and Goldman, between the rounds, was looking very serious as he talked to his pupil. Also, he was working on Rocky's brows with cotton-tipped toothpicks that had been steeped in some astringent solution. The jabs had cut. But Rocky came out for each new round very gay, as Egan would say, and went across to Louis as if to ask for a light.

When the fifth round ended, marking the halfway point of the fight, I felt that it would be a long way home but that Louis would make it. He had hardly used his left hook, which was now his best punch. Critics had been saying for years that his right had lost its authority, but the hook had existed in all its pristine glory as recently as the Savold bout, and he had had it in the training camp when I was watching him. ("It would take a Goliath to withstand a couple of those," old Colonel Stingo had said solemnly.) The way I figured it, Louis was being so careful about that crazy Marciano right that he was afraid to pull his own left back to hook. He would just jab and drop his forearm onto Rocky's right biceps, so he couldn't counter. Sooner or later, Joe would throw the hook, I thought, and that would end the fight. It looked like a fight between two men with one good hand apiece.

In the sixth, things started to go sour. It wasn't that Marciano grew better or stronger; it was that Louis seemed to get slower and weaker. The spring was gone from his legs—and it had been only a slight spring in the beginning—and in the clinches Marciano was shoving him around. A man can be as strong for tugging and hauling at thirty-seven, or for that matter at forty-seven, as he was in his twenties, but he can't keep on starting and stopping for as many minutes. And even grazing blows begin to hurt after a while. Near the end of the round, Marciano hit Louis another solid one.

The seventh was bad for Louis. Marciano didn't catch him with one big punch, but he was battering at his body and arms, and shoving him around, and Joe didn't seem to be able to do anything about it. Then, toward the end of the round, Joe threw the hook. It was beautiful. It hit Marciano flush on the right side of the jaw, but it didn't seem to faze him a bit. I knew then that Joe was beaten, but I thought that it might be only a decision. Three rounds don't seem forever, especially when you're just watching.

Then, in the eighth round, as you probably read in the daily press, Marciano, the right-hand specialist, knocked Louis down with a left hook that Goldman had not previously publicized. When Louis got up, Marciano hit him with two more left hooks, which set him up for the right and the pitiful finish.

Right after Marciano knocked Louis down the first time, Sugar Ray Robinson started working his way toward the ring, as if drawn by some horrid fascination, and by the time Rocky threw the final right, Robinson's hand was on the lowest rope of the ring, as if he meant to jump in. The punch knocked Joe through the ropes and he lay on the ring apron, only one leg inside.

The tall blonde was bawling, and pretty soon she began to sob. The fellow who had brought her was horrified. "Rocky didn't do anything wrong," he said. "He didn't foul him. What you booing?"

The blonde said, "You're so cold. I hate you, too."

Two weeks later, I stopped by the offices of the International Boxing Club to ask Al Weill how he felt about things now. "What did I tell you?" he said. "You want to look out for them broken fighters. The way things look now, the kid could make a fortune of money."

The Melting Middleweight

SUGAR RAY AND THE MILLING COVE

PART of the pleasure of going to a fight is reading the newspapers next morning to see what the sports writers think happened. This pleasure is prolonged, in the case of a big bout, by the fight films. You can go to them to see what *did* happen. What you eventually think you remember about the fight will be an amalgam of what you thought you saw there, what you read in the papers you saw, and what you saw in the films.

The films are especially insidious. During the last twenty seconds or so of the fight between Sugar Ray Robinson and Randy Turpin, for example, it seemed to me from where I sat, in the lower stand at the Polo Grounds, that Robinson hit the failing Turpin with every blow he threw—a succession of smashing hits such as I had never before seen a fighter take without going down. The films show that Robinson missed quite a few of them, and that Turpin, although not able to hit back, was putting up some defensive action until the last second—swaying low, with his gloves shielding his sad face, gray-white in the films. It was the face of a schoolboy who has long trained himself not to cry under punishment and who has had endless chances to practice, like an inmate of Dotheboys Hall. That's the way I now catch myself remembering Turpin's face in the last seconds, although I couldn't see it at the Polo Grounds because Robinson was between us and both were a good distance from me anyway. The face isn't gray-white in real life, but a kind of dun.

The films of the first nine rounds of the fight upset my original impressions in the same way. Those rounds seem exciting now, because I look for hints of what is to come in the tenth, which contained all the fight's excitement. I forget that when they were being fought I saw them only as nine very bad rounds, almost a hoax on the 61,370 spectators, who, in the consecrated formula, had paid $767,630 for the privilege of watching them. All they seemed likely to lead to was six more bad rounds and a decision that would be sure to provoke an argument, since the boxers were going nowhere at the same pace. In the third, or maybe the fourth, round, the fans in the general-admission seats began to clap in unison, as they do at small clubs when two preliminary boys either can't or won't fight. I wondered if either Robinson or Turpin had ever before been treated so disrespectfully. Their styles seemed just made to reduce each other to absurdity. But years from now, when I reminisce about the fight, I'll probably say it was tense all the way, and I'll believe it.

I still think the referee, Ruby Goldstein, was right to stop the fight; no referee should take it upon himself to gamble on a man's recuperative powers. One more punch like the ones Robinson was throwing might have ended the boxing days of any fighter—even Turpin, who is what *Boxiana* would have called "a prime glutton." *Boxiana* is one of my favorite books, and, because of the international nature of the fight, I had a refresher glance at it before going up to the Polo Grounds.

On the night of the fight I started out early, in the true Egan tradition. In his time, the migration to a fight would begin days in advance, when the foot-toddlers (fellows who couldn't afford horse-drawn transportation) would set out on the road for the rumored meeting place. Rumors were all they had to go on because in England at that time prizefighting, although patronized by the Prince Regent, was illegal. A day or so later, the milling coves and the flash coves (fighters and knowing boys) would set out in wagons or hackneys, with plenty of Cyprians and blue ruin (sporting girls and gin) to keep them happy on their way. The Cyprians counted on making new and more profitable connections later. Last of all, the Corinthians (amateurs of the fancy and patrons of pugilists) would take the road in their fast traps and catch up with the others in time to get their bets down before the fight. But blue ruin stopped many a wagon before it got there; milling coves and flash coves both were lushing coves.

Attendance at an old-time British fight was preceded, for all classes, by a visit to the pubs of the contending heros, to wish them success. In accordance with this tradition, at six o'clock on the evening of the Robinson-Turpin fight I made my way to Sugar Ray's, which is Robinson's pub, on the west side of Seventh Avenue between 123rd and 124th Streets.

Improvements in transportation have made it unnecessary to start for a fight days in advance, unless one is to foot-toddle. I approached the pub by taxi, the equivalent of a hackney, but sans Cyprian, and disembarked on the northeast corner of Seventh Avenue and 124th Street, in front of the Citadel of Hope Mission, which was not getting much of a play. I got out there because if I'd got out on the Robinson side of the street I'd have had to step on somebody's feet. With the time to go to the fight drawing near, the sidewalk in front of his bar-and-grill had vanished. The sidewalk in front of the Hotel Theresa, which extends from 124th to 125th Street on the west side of Seventh Avenue, was similarly jammed with Harlemites, and the narrow traffic island in the middle of the avenue was also filled with Negroes, who were gazing up at the hotel.

A small colored boy, presumably from the Citadel of Hope, handed me a throwaway preaching class war. "There are two classes of people in the world—the righteous and the wicked," it read. "You belong to one of these two classes. Which?"

"Let me ask you a question," I said to the boy. "Who is up in that hotel?"

"Randy," the boy answered. "He's resting until the fight."

I looked about me and imagined the trade consequences of a Turpin victory. I could visualize the thousands of shoulders draped in British tweed, and the equal number of feet, now impacted one on another, encased in shoes by Maxwell of Dover Street. In Harlem, fashion follows the brave. It seemed to me I could already detect a slight premonitory change, in the accent of the first man who spoke to me, but he may have been a West Indian. "Randy is superior," he said. "He's overconfi-*dence*. I mean he feel no fear."

I crossed the street and worked my way into the lobby of the Theresa, which is the largest hotel under Negro management in America and about the busiest hotel anywhere—a contrast to its moribund last twenty years in white hands. Joe Louis was standing, almost unnoticed, with a group of friends near the door. He's still a favorite, but no novelty. Everybody was waiting for a look at Randy.

Coming out of the Theresa, I stood on the inner edge of the sidewalk and allowed myself to be propelled slowly half a block downtown, being carried past the Golden Glovers' Barber-shop and the store-front office of Ray Robinson Enterprises. (Robinson is in almost as many businesses in Harlem as Father Divine was before that divinity moved to Philadelphia.) I detached myself from the current just in time to duck into Sugar Ray's, which is a narrow but deep saloon with walls of blue glass chips tastefully picked out with gold. The bar was as crowded as the street outside, but at the back of the place, where the bar ends, Sugar Ray's widens out enough to permit three parallel rows of tables, one row against each side wall and the third between them, and there were a few empty seats. Since I could find no place to stand up, I sat down at a table.

This rear section of Sugar Ray's is decorated with four huge photomontages, two on each side wall. Two show him making a fool of Kid Gavilan, the Cuban fighter, who is a competitor of his for local fame. Another shows Robinson bringing an expression of intensely comic pain to the face of the French middle-weight Robert Villemain, a muscle-bound, pyknic type with a square head. The fourth shows him standing above Georgie Abrams, a skillful pugilist who is so hairy that when knocked down he looks like a rug. Abrams got up after his knockdown, but from the picture it doesn't seem as if he ever would.

I asked a man at the table next to mine, who looked like an old colored milling cove, whether the boss was around, and he said he wasn't. "He left about an hour ago," he said. "He's taking this one serious. He was carrying his bag, and I told him, 'Now, don't you stop on the way to do any training.'" Some women at the cove's table laughed, and so did I. I dined on bourbon and the largest, pinkest pork chops I have ever seen, priced at a dollar-sixty-five. "They're mighty good," I said to the cove, who seemed to be regarding me with interest. "They ought to be," he said. "I once fought a man eight rounds for not much more than that."

I approved of Robinson's decision to leave early. Drinking with customers just before a battle was a practice deprecated by Egan. There was, to give you an example from *Boxiana*, Dan Donnelly, an Irish heavyweight, who was never beaten but who fell dead in his own bar after drinking forty-seven whiskey punches with well-wishers. His epitaph read:

O'ERTHROWN BY PUNCH,
UNHARMED BY FIST,
HE DIED UNBEATEN PUGILIST!

A slim, earnest black man with a briar pipe in his right hand walked down between the tables, saying in a peremptory voice, "A hundred to seventy-five. A hundred to seventy-five." "*What* you betting?" another man asked him. "I bet Robinson," the man with the pipe said. "Everybody here betting him," the second man said. "That ain't no odds." The man with the pipe walked away, and I asked the second man, "Who do you think will win?" "Ray," he said. "Ray, sure. He always win when the chips are down." I did not tell him about the statement of Colonel Stingo, whom I had encountered the day before and who had seen the films of the London bout in which Turpin defeated Robinson for the middleweight championship. The Colonel said Turpin appeared to be a very strong boxer, and had kept crowding Robinson from the beginning of the bout. "Ray has never looked too good against a crowding fighter," the Colonel said, "and now he's getting old. He's got to make a different kind of a fight to win this one." He added that he had just been talking to Jack Kearns, the former manager of Jack Dempsey. Kearns had been out to Pompton Lakes to watch Sugar Ray train, and had said that he was "dry"—not sweating well—which is considered an indication of poor condition. "It'll take him a year to get back in shape," Kearns had told the Colonel. "Paris licked him."

When I arrived at the Polo Grounds, a short time before the first preliminary bout, the place was only half full, but the people running the show had already effected an almost complete strangulation of movement as far as the customers were concerned. By setting up wire gates between various sections of the stand, probably to prevent ticket holders from "creeping" forward to better seats than they had paid for, they had made long detours necessary for anyone trying to get anywhere. Since even the ushers, of whom there were few, didn't know where the temporary barriers were, they couldn't tell people how to avoid them. A lane so narrow that it could be threaded only in single file had been left between the lower-stand boxes and the first row of lower-stand seats, and customers coming in through runways at the ends of this lane had to struggle against each other to reach the aisles leading up into the stands. Once I had made it to my own seat, in the first row of the lower stand, the struggle provided a sort of preliminary to the preliminaries.

The "ringside" seats, which covered the baseball diamond and reached well into the outfield, were for the most part empty at that stage of the evening. They filled slowly; many of the people who buy them do not much like boxing but go to big fights so that they can talk about them afterward, and they seldom arrive before the main bout. But I knew they would be along; this was something you had to see, like *Guys and Dolls* or a van Gogh show at the Metropolitan. Midway through the preliminaries, hundreds of young hoodlums in Hawaiian shirts, all of whom had clearly come in on general admission—unless they had scaled the fence—dashed down the aisles of the stands in back of third base, vaulted the wire barriers with admirable ease, and hurtled onto the field, racing to occupy empty ringside seats. It was a concerted break, and there weren't nearly enough special cops to stop them. Once in a seat, each of these fellows would try to avoid attention until the rightful ticket holder arrived, upon which, after a conversational delaying action, the interloper would move to another empty seat, continuing to move until the lights went out for the main bout. Then, if evicted again, he would squat in an aisle. The specials were flushing them all through the show, in a succession of comedy chases. The rush, because it was so concerted, did not amuse me; in a previous decade and in other circumstances, the louts might have been wearing black or brown shirts, I thought, and a time might come when they would be again. The night was sweating hot.

I could identify one ticket holder who was already in his seat. He was a man who looks like Ethel Waters, especially when he has his mouth open, and who calls himself Prince Monolulu. He says he is an Ethiopian prince, and wears a bright-red jacket embroidered with the Star of David and the signs of the zodiac, as well as a headdress of ostrich plumes and a set of flowing skirts. These make him fairly easy to recognize if you have seen him once, and I had seen him several times in

England—once at Epsom, plying his regular trade as a race-track tout, and on endless Sundays at Hyde Park Corner, where he preaches Zionism. I had read in the morning paper that he'd come over on a chartered plane with fifty other Turpin supporters. When working, Prince Monolulu shouts, at unpleasantly frequent intervals, "I got a 'orse!" and then, to those who gather around in response to his shouts, he tells about the dialogue between the camiknickers and the night-gown, winding up by selling his horse, on a folded slip of paper, for a modest half crown. I bought Black Tarquin from him at Epsom, and it beat twenty-four other horses, finishing eighth. At the Polo Grounds, I noticed, he was silent. He may have been molting.

In the very first preliminary, one boy knocked the other down for a count of nine in the first round, and the referee stopped the fight. This apparently exaggerated solicitude, I felt sure, could be attributed to the death of a preliminary fighter named Georgie Flores, who had been fatally injured when knocked out in Madison Square Garden a couple of weeks earlier.

In another preliminary Jackie Turpin, an older brother of the champion's and a featherweight, defeated a boy named Wams-ley in six rounds. Jackie is a light tan, like his bigger brother, but on the night of this fight the resemblance ended there. I thought he boxed a bit like Jackie (Kid) Berg, an English light-weight of the thirties, getting inside fast and throwing dozens of punches, most of which landed but none of which seemed solid. Still, the other boy went down for short counts twice, and Turpin earned the decision. I knew that somewhere in the stands there were five hundred members of the Queen Eliza-beth's crew, and the cheering for the featherweight Turpin showed where they were sitting—behind the third-base line.

The semifinal was between two big Negro heavyweights, one of whom, apparently beaten, knocked the other out in the last thirty seconds. "How do you like that?" one of two Garment Center Corinthians on my right asked his companion. "Just before he landed the winning punch, he was supremely out."

Then the ring was full of fighters, the majority of them colored, being introduced to the crowd, and the belated ringside-seat holders were pouring in, a number of pretty women with them. Jersey Joe Walcott, then the heavyweight champion; Ezzard Charles, his predecessor; and Joe Louis entered the ring together and were introduced, one at a time; Louis got an ovation, although he was then just the champion-before-last. (When he walked out on the field to his seat before the semifinal, he was given a bigger hand than General MacArthur, who preceded him.) Louis looks like a champion and carries himself like a champion, and people will continue to call him champion as long as he lives.

The two seats at my left, which had been vacant all evening, were now occupied by a couple. The girl, a smashing blonde in a backless black evening dress, must have expected that she was going to sit out in ringside, where people could see her. A woman somewhere behind her said, but not to her, "I call that a vulgar way to dress." It seemed to cheer the blonde, but the man with her looked uncomfortable.

Everybody stood up for a long recorded version of "God Save the King," with a vocal chorus. It reminded me of the time they played the "Marseillaise" for Marcel Cerdan before he knocked out Tony Zale in Jersey City, and the machine wouldn't stop. "God Save the King" received polite applause. The applause for "The Star-Spangled Banner," which followed it, was tumultuous.

The principals came into the ring. Robinson, the challenger, was first—tall, slender, and dark brown, wearing a blue-and-white robe. He discarded the robe, revealing white trunks with a blue stripe, and jigged furiously up and down to limber his leg muscles. Turpin followed, in a yellow bathrobe over black trunks with a white stripe, sat down in his corner, and remained seated, even during the introduction, while Robinson stood and waved to the crowd. Robinson acted like a young, nervous fighter; Turpin, eight years his junior and fighting for the first time in this country, was calm as a Colchester oyster. When the bell rang, it was the same way. Robinson was making the play. Turpin wasn't crowding this time; he was taking it easy, as if sure Robinson would slow down. Jimmy Cannon, of the New York *Post*, wrote afterward that Turpin "moved with a clumsy spryness and appeared to be serenely anticipating Robinson's collapse." The trouble with this policy was that it gave the much older Robinson a chance to make his own pace, fighting in spurts and then resting. He was still about the fastest thing in the world for thirty seconds or so, as Turpin was to find out.

Turpin stood more like some of the illustrations of boxers in *Boxiana* than a modern fighter. He had his left knee far forward, the leg almost straight out, and all the weight of his body back. It made him hard to get at, but it also made it hard for him to get at Robinson. (I had often wondered, looking at those illustrations, how men could hit from that position. Now I understand why *Boxiana* lists so many fifty- and sixty-round fights.) When Turpin did hit—with marvelous speed, most of which was wasted in coming such a long way around —it was always at some curious angle. One punch for the body looked like a man releasing a bowling ball; another, a right for the head, was like a granny boxing a boy's ears. His jab was like a man starting his run for the pole vault. If he hit conventionally, from the shoulder, he would be less disconcerting, but he might also be one of the hardest hitters in history. For he is the strongest middleweight I have ever seen—built like a heavyweight, and tall, too. I haven't figured yet how he can be so big all around and still make a hundred and sixty pounds.

Turpin was so strong that his unconventional blows shook Robinson when they landed, although Robinson knew that, according to the book, they shouldn't. When the warning whistle blew ten seconds before the beginning of the second round, Robinson stood up. I thought it a rash gesture, because it meant that now he would have to spend an extra ten seconds on his feet at every interval. If he stayed down, it would be a public confession that he was tired. Turpin sat the full minute.

"The kid's got nothin', nothin', absolutely nothin'," one of the fellows next to me began saying during the fifth or sixth round, meaning Turpin, and he continued to repeat it, like an incantation: "Nothin', nothin'." He must have had a good bet on Robinson, because he sounded worried.

"If Turpin hasn't got anything, what's Robinson got?" I finally asked him. "It's even, isn't it?"

"Even?" He looked at me as if I were mad. "Turpin ain't took a round," he said.

The referee's card had four rounds for each fighter and one even, up to the tenth round.

A stout colored man in back of me was wearing a bright-green suit, a Tattersall waistcoat with a green stripe, a yellow tie, and a maroon silk shirt with two-inch white polka dots. If he had taken off jacket, waistcoat, and about forty pounds, he would have been dressed to ride for the Woolford Farm Stable, of Kansas City, Missouri. Every time Sugar Ray started a punch, this man would grunt like a bullfrog and then softly moan, as if enduring the agony of a shattered Turpin, even when the punch didn't land.

I was beginning to resent my neighbors bitterly by the time the tenth round came and Robinson, with his eye cut, either by a butt or by a blow, put together the really amazing attack that finished poor Turpin off—or didn't quite, according, next day, to Turpin's manager and to some of the British boxing writers, who hadn't been hit. When the referee stepped between the fighters and grabbed Turpin in his arms, I thought I had never seen a man so game or so beaten as the mulatto from Leamington Spa. Within a minute, the ring was full of police-men, who lined the ropes; I don't exactly know why, since there appeared to be no danger of a riot. There seemed to be nothing to argue about.

On the way down the ramp to the exit, I saw a sight that struck the proper note—a tall, grave, fair-haired man, with a pipe in his mouth, walking silently beside an equally grave blond boy of around fifteen, who was carrying a furled Union Jack. By contrast, as I got out onto Eighth Avenue, under the "El," I nearly bumped into three men who turned out to be sailors from the Elizabeth, and though they were wearing Turpin buttons in the lapels of their land-going clothes, they were all laughing. "I feel like 'iding my fice," one of them was saying. "What a 'iding 'e took!" "What I'm laughing at," said another, "was old Bill, 'ere. 'Go right in, Randy,' 'e says. 'What are you afraid of?'" They were, I felt, devoid of proper patriotic sentiment.

Since there were no taxis to be had and the subway en-trances, choked with struggling human bodies, looked slightly less inviting in that heat than gas chambers, I started to foot-toddle down Eighth Avenue, hoping to encounter a cab along

the way. After I'd gone a block or so, I was stopped by another
British seaman, a square-faced bloke who looked as if he might
once have boxed a bit himself. He wanted to know the way to
the entrance to the Eighth Avenue subway I had just passed
up. I told him, and added consolingly, "I never saw a gamer
man than your fellow." "Oh, 'im," the seaman said. "'E's a
good lad, sir, but no experience. No defense. No class, sir. Forget about 'im." This, too, seemed hardly right.

Eighth Avenue, from the Polo Grounds south, is Harlem,
but it's poor Harlem, unrelieved by bright lights or jive. I
walked past store fronts fetid with the smell of old vegetables,
and dismal houses that never were much and now are less,
where ill-dressed Negroes sat on the doorsills. Other people
walking from the fight, or perhaps a radio bulletin, had carried
the news ahead of me. (The fight itself, of course, hadn't been
broadcast or televised—for New York audiences, at any rate.)
All along the way, the people in the doorways knew that Sugar
Ray had won, but they didn't seem excited. Perhaps it was the
heat.

I stopped in at a bar at 145th Street for a drink—it was not
festive there, either—and then switched over to Seventh Avenue,
still looking for a taxi. At 143rd and Seventh, two men in their
twenties were bullying a boy of about eighteen. They had him
backed up against an automobile, and whenever he turned on
one, the other would kick him. A crowd of women had gathered
around, at a safe distance. The men had been drinking and
looked rough. "You let him alone!" a woman cried. "He's only
a young boy!" In a nearby saloon, there was another row
going on. Just then, I sighted a cab headed uptown empty, and
I stopped it and got aboard. "Drive me downtown, past Sugar
Ray's," I said.

As we approached the Theresa, the avenue was so jammed
up with traffic that we could barely move. People were packed
around the safety islands and overflowed onto the street. Somebody was beating an oilcan like a tomtom, and a tall, limber
man was dancing in the street. Any idea I may have had of
stopping at Sugar Ray's for a nightcap left me when I saw the
crowd in front of the door.

My maid walked by Sugar Ray's a couple of days after the
fight, and she said there were twenty-five Cadillacs parked in

front of the place. "Any that weren't 1951 had to double-park," she said. "His is a big pink one. He was standing outside, with just a small patch over his eye, and everybody that came by shook hands with him."

I went up to Sugar Ray's myself on the following Sunday, but it was very quiet, with only a girl about five feet tall behind the bar, and a monumental cash register and a sign that read, "Try Sugar Ray's Bolo, 55 cents." The bolo, which is named after one of Robinson's favorite punches, is made of rum. There were enough customers to keep the girl busy, but they all looked tired, as if they had been celebrating for several nights in a row and had just come in for pick-me-ups.

KEARNS BY A KNOCKOUT

The division of boxers into weight classes is based on the premise that if two men are equally talented practitioners of the Sweet Science, then the heavier man has a decided advantage. This is true, of course, only if both men are trained down hard, since a pound of beer is of no use in a boxing match. If the difference amounts to no more than a couple of pounds, it can be offset by a number of other factors, including luck, but when it goes up to five or six or seven, it takes a lot of beating. The span between the top limit of one weight class and the next represents the margin that history has proved is almost impossible to overcome. Between middleweight and light heavyweight, for example, that gap is fifteen pounds. A middleweight champion may weigh, at the most, a hundred and sixty, and a light heavy a hundred and seventy-five. But some champions are more skillful than others, and every now and then one comes along who feels he can beat the title-holder in the class above him. That was what made it interesting to anticipate the match between Sugar Ray Robinson, the middleweight champion, and Joey Maxim, the champion of the light heavyweights, in June, 1952. As soon as I heard the match had been arranged, I resolved to attend it. I had seen Robinson in four fights, not including television, and knew that he was a very good fighter. I had heard that Maxim, whom I had never seen, was merely pretty good. But there was that fifteen pounds. It was the smaller man who appealed to the public's imagination, and to mine. Goliath would not have been a popular champion even if he had flattened David in the first round. Robinson is such a combination of skill and grace that I had a feeling he could do the trick. For exactly the same reason, the London fancy, back in 1821, made Tom Hickman, the Gas-Light Man, who weighed a hundred and sixty-five, a strong favorite over Bill Neat, at a hundred and eighty-nine. The Gas-Light Man, according to Egan, was "a host within himself—his fist possessing the knocking-down force of the forge-hammer— his brow contemptuously smiling at defeat—*to surrender* not within the range of his ideas, even to the extremity of perspective—and VICTORY, proud victory, only operating as a beacon to all his achievements." Neat was a mere plugger, but he "turned out the Gas."

One man who did not share the public's sentimental regard for Robinson was an old-time prizefighter, saloon-keeper, and manufacturer of fire extinguishers named Jack Kearns. This was not surprising, because Kearns, who in more glorious eras managed Jack Dempsey, the Manassa Mauler, and Mickey Walker, the Toy Bulldog, now happens to be the manager of Maxim. Not even Kearns hinted that Maxim was a great champion, but he said he had a kind nature. "All he lacks is the killer instinct," Jack maintained. "But he takes a good punch. When he's knocked down he always gets up." He once told a group of fight writers, "Maxim is as good a fighter as Dempsey, except he can't hit." Since that was all Dempsey could do, Kearns wasn't handing his new man much.

Kearns is as rutilant a personality as Maxim apparently isn't, and from many of the newspaper stories that appeared in the weeks leading up to the fight one would have thought that Kearns, not Maxim, was signed to fight Robinson. This was an impression Kearns seemed to share when I met him six days before the date set for the fight, in the large, well-refrigerated Broadway restaurant operated by his former associate Dempsey. The old champion and his manager quarreled spectacularly back in the twenties, but are now friendly. "This is my big chance," Kearns said, buying me a drink and ordering a cup of coffee for himself. He was one of the big speakeasy spenders but says he has been on the wagon for eight years. "Up to now, I had to stuff myself up and fight heavyweights," he said. "Me, the only white guy with a title. But now I got somebody I can bull around." By this he meant, I gathered, that, in order to obtain what he considered sufficiently remunerative employment in the past for Maxim, he had had to overfeed the poor fellow and spread the rumor that he had grown into a full-sized heavyweight. Then, after fattening him to a hundred and eighty, he had exposed him to the assault of more genuine giants, who had nearly killed him. But now, he implied, Maxim had an opponent he could shove around and control in the clinches. I said I hoped it would be a good fight to watch, and he said, "I got to be good. I can't afford to lay back. I got to keep moving him, moving him." As he said this, he picked off imaginary punches—Robinson's hooks, no doubt—with both hands and shoved straight out into space, to show how he would put on the pressure.

Most managers say "we" will lick So-and-So when they mean their man will try to, but Kearns does not allow his fighter even a share in the pronoun. He is a manager of the old school. His old-school tie, on the day I met him, was Columbia blue covered with sharps and flats in black, green, and cerise. The weaver of his shirt had imprisoned in it the texture as well as the color of pistachio ice cream. It was a wonder children hadn't eaten it off his back in the street, with the weather the way it was outside. He was wearing a pale-gray suit and skewbald shoes, and his eyes, of a confiding baby blue, were so bright that they seemed a part of the ensemble. He has a long, narrow, pink face that widens only at the cheekbones and at the mouth, which is fronted with wide, friendly-looking incisors, habitually exposed in an ingenuous smile. The big ears folded back against the sides of his head are not cauliflowered. They are evidence that in his boxing days he was never a catcher. Kearns is slim and active, and could pass for a spry fifty-five if the record books didn't show that he was knocked out by a welterweight champion named Honey Mellody in 1901, when he must have been at least full-grown.

In the course of his boxing career, which was not otherwise distinguished, Kearns had the fortune to meet the two fighters who in my opinion had the best ring names of all time—Honey

Melody and Mysterious Billy Smith. Smith was also a welterweight champion. "He was always doing something mysterious," Kearns says. "Like he would step on your foot, and when you looked down, he would bite you in the ear. If I had a fighter like that now, I could lick heavyweights. But we are living in a bad period all around. The writers are always crabbing about the fighters we got now, but look at the writers you got now themselves. All they think about is home to wife and children, instead of laying around saloons soaking up information."

He told me in Dempsey's that he played nine holes of golf every day to keep his legs in shape. Since Kearns was obviously in such good condition, I saw no point in taking the three-hour ride to Grossinger's, in the Catskill Mountains, to see Maxim train.

I did go out to look at Robinson next day, however. He was training at Pompton Lakes, New Jersey, which is only an hour's drive from town. I got a free ride in one of the limousines chartered by the International Boxing Club, which was promoting the fight. There were four newspapermen with me, including a fellow named Frank Butler, from the *News of the World*, of London, who had seen both Robinson and Maxim fight in England and said Maxim could bash a bit when he liked. "He took all Freddie Mills' front teeth out with one uppercut," he said. "I rather think he'll do Robinson."

Any effect Mr. Butler's prediction might have had on me was dissipated by the atmosphere of the camp. When we arrived, a crowd had already gathered around George Gainford, Robinson's immense, impressive manager, on the lawn between the sleeping quarters and the press building. It was a mass interview. The topic of discussion was what Robinson was going to do with *two* championships after he whipped Maxim. Since Robinson would indubitably weigh under a hundred and seventy-five pounds for the fight, the light heavyweight title would be his if he won. But since Maxim would certainly weigh more than a hundred and sixty, he could not take the middleweight championship, no matter what he did to Robinson. The chairman of the New York State Athletic Commission, someone said to Gainford, had announced that if Robinson won the heavier championship, he would have to abandon the lighter one. It sounded to me like the kind of hypothetical problem harried publicity men so often cook up as fight day approaches. But Gainford, a vast ebon man, broad between the eyes, played it straight. "The Commission do not make a champion," he intoned. "Neither may the Supreme Court name him. The people of the world name him; that is democracy. And if Robinson emerge victorious, he will be champion in both classes until somebody defeat him."

"How about the welterweight championship?" somebody asked. Robinson was the welterweight champion (one hundred and forty-seven pounds) until he entered the middleweight class. He was never beaten at that weight.

"I do not want to make that weight," Gainford said majestically, using the first person singular as if he were Jack Kearns. He must weigh two hundred and forty.

While Gainford propounded, the fighter and three campmates were sitting around a table, unperturbed by the jostling visitors. They were playing hearts, and all shouting simultaneously that they were being cheated. Robinson put an end to the game by standing up and saying he had better get ready for his workout. He was wearing a green-and-white straw cap and a red-and-white Basque shirt and cinnamon slacks, and he looked as relaxed and confident as a large Siamese tomcat. Sam Taub, the I.B.C. press agent at the camp, led him into the press shack to be interviewed by "just the bona-fide newspapermen," and he sprawled gracefully on a narrow typewriter shelf, one leg straight out and the other dangling. Robinson is about six feet in length, very tall for a middleweight, and on casual inspection he seems more like a loose-limbed dancer than a boxer. A long, thin neck, the customary complement of long arms and legs, is a disadvantage to a boxer, because a man with his head attached that way doesn't take a good punch. The great layer of muscle on the back of Robinson's neck is the outward indication of his persistence. It is the kind that can be developed only by endless years of exercise—the sort of exercise no shiftless man will stick with.

"Have you ever fought a man that heavy?" a newspaperman asked him.

"Never a *champion* that heavy," Robinson said, smiling.

"Do you think you can hurt him?" the man asked.

"I can hurt anybody," the boxer said. "Can I hurt him enough is the question. I'll be hitting *at* him, all right."

"Have you a plan for the battle?" another fellow asked.

"If you have a plan, the other fellow is liable to do just the opposite," Robinson said.

"How are your legs?" somebody else asked.

"I hope they all right," Robinson said. "This would sure be a bad time for them to go wrong."

The interview broke up and the fighter went along to get into his ring togs. He worked four easy rounds with two partners, who didn't seem to want to irritate him. They sparred outdoors, in a ring on a kind of bandstand under the trees. Around the ring were bleachers, occupied by a couple of hundred spectators—Harlem people and visiting prizefighters and a busload of boys brought out from the city by the Police Athletic League. "We had three hundred paid admissions at a buck here last Sunday," Taub told me. "Sugar gave a dinner for sixty-five. 'My friends and relatives,' he said. They ate fifty-five chickens."

The newspapermen agreed that tepid sparring was all right, since Sugar Ray was as sharp as a tack already, and this was almost the end of his training. The thing about Robinson that gets you is the way he moves, even when shadowboxing. He finished off with a good long session of jumping rope, which he enjoys. Most fighters jump rope as children do, but infinitely faster. Robinson just swings a length of rope in his right fist and jumps in time to a fast tune whistled by his trainer. He jumps high in the air, and twists his joined knees at the top of every bound. When he jumps in double time to "I'm Just Wild About Harry," it's really something to see.

On the way back to town we all said he had never looked better.

The fight itself, as you have probably read, was memorable, but chiefly for meteorological reasons. It was postponed from the night of Monday, June twenty-third to that of Wednesday, June twenty-fifth, because of rain. Wednesday was the hottest June twenty-fifth in the history of the New York City Weather Bureau. I rode the subway up to the Yankee Stadium, where the fight was to be held, and the men slumped in the seats and hanging to the straps weren't talking excitedly or making jokes, as fight fans generally do. They were just gasping gently, like fish that had been caught two hours earlier. Most of those who had been wearing neckties had removed them, but rings of red and green remained around collars and throats to show the color of the ties that had been there. Shirts stuck to the folds of bellies, and even the floor was wet with sweat.

My seat was in a mezzanine box on the first-base line, and I felt a mountain climber's exhaustion by the time I had ascended the three gentle inclines that lead to the top of the grandstand, from which I had to descend to my seat. A fellow in a party behind me, trying to cheer his companions, said, "And you can tell your grandsons about this fight and how hot it was." The preliminaries were on when I arrived, and two wretched forms were hacking away at each other under the lights that beat down on the ring. I could see the high shine on the wringing-wet bodies, and imagined that each man must be praying to be knocked out as speedily as possible. They were too inept; the bout went the full distance of six rounds, and then both men collapsed in their corners, indifferent to the decision. A miasma of cigarette smoke hung over the "ringside" seats on the baseball diamond, producing something of the effect you get when you fly over a cloud bank. There was no breeze to dispel it, and the American flags on the four posts at the corners of the ring drooped straight down. It was a hundred and four degrees Fahrenheit in there, we were to learn from the newspapers next morning.

I missed the next two preliminaries because I was up at the top of the stand, waiting in line for a can of beer. The venders who usually swarm all over the place, obstructing your vision at crucial moments in a fight, had disappeared, on the one night when their presence would have been welcome. So the customers had to queue up—a death march to get to a bar tended by exactly two men. Meanwhile, the fights were invisible, but once one was locked in the line, the thought of giving up one's place unslaked became intolerable. Our line inched along toward a kind of Storm Trooper with a head like a pink egg. Rivulets of sweat poured from the watershed of his cranium, and his face appeared behind a spray, like a bronze Triton's in a fountain. At every third customer, he would stop the line and threaten to pack up and call it a day. We would look at him beseechingly, too thirsty even to protest, and after enjoying our humiliation for a while he would consent to sell more beer.

By the time I got back to my seat, Robinson and Maxim were in the ring and the announcer was proceeding with the usual tiresome introductions of somebodies who were going to fight somebody elses somewhere. Each boy, after being introduced, would walk over and touch the gloved right paw of each principal. The last one in was old Jersey Joe Walcott, the heavyweight champion, and the crowd evidenced torpid good will. I could see the vast Gainford in Robinson's corner, over toward third base, and, with the aid of binoculars, could discern that his face still wore the portentous, noncommittal expression of a turbaned bishop in a store-front church. Kearns had his back to me, but I could tell him by his ears. He was clad in a white T shirt with "Joey Maxim" in dark letters on the back, and he seemed brisker than anybody else in the ring. Maxim had his back to me, too. When he stood up, I could see how much thicker and broader through the chest he was than Robinson. His skin was a reddish bronze; Sugar Ray's was mocha chocolate.

Fighting middleweights, Robinson had always had a superiority over his foes in height and reach, together with equality in weight. Against Maxim he had equality in height and reach but the weight was all against him. His was announced as a hundred fifty-seven and a half and Maxim's as a hundred and seventy-three. The first ten rounds of the fight weren't much to watch. Maxim would keep walking in and poking a straight left at Robinson's face. Robinson would either take or slip it, according to his fortune, belt Maxim a couple of punches, and grab his arms. Then they would contend, with varying success, in close. Some of the fans would cry that Robinson wasn't hurting Maxim at all in these interludes, others that Maxim wasn't hurting Robinson at all. There seemed to be some correlation between their eyesight and where they had placed their money. Because of the nature of the combat, most of the work fell upon the referee, Ruby Goldstein, a former welterweight then in his forties, who had to pull the men apart. In consequence, he was the first of the three to collapse; he had to leave the ring after the tenth round. I have never seen this happen in a prizefight before. Old-time photographs show referees on their feet at the end of twenty-five-round fights, and wearing waistcoats and stiff collars. It is a bad period all around.

Robinson had been hitting Maxim much more frequently than Maxim had been hitting him, but neither man seemed hurt, and both were slowing down from a pace that had never been brisk. Now the relief referee, Ray Miller, a snub-nosed little man with reddish hair, entered the ring, bringing with him more bounce than either of the contestants possessed. He must have been sitting on dry ice. Miller, also an old fighter, enjoined the fighters to get going. The crowd had begun clapping and stamping, midway in the fight, to manifest its boredom. Miller broke clinches so expeditiously in the eleventh and twelfth that the pace increased slightly, to the neighborhood of a fast creep. Up to then, it had been even worse than the first ten rounds of the previous year's fight between Sugar Ray and Randy Turpin, the milling cove. But that fight had ended in one wildly exciting round that made the fancy forget how dull the prelude had been.

This fight was to produce excitement, too, but of a fantastically different kind. In the eleventh round, Robinson hit Maxim precisely the same kind of looping right to the jaw that had started Turpin on the way out. The blow knocked the light heavy clear across the ring, but he didn't fall, and Robinson's legs, those miracles, apparently couldn't move Ray fast enough to take advantage of the situation. It may have been as good a punch as the one of the year before, but it landed on a man fifteen pounds heavier. Maxim shook his head and went right on fighting, in his somnambulistic way. Now all Sugar Ray had to do was finish the fight on his feet and he would win on points. But when he came out for the thirteenth, he walked as if he had the gout in both feet and dreaded putting them down. When he punched, which was infrequently, he was as late, and as wild, as an amateur, and when he wasn't punching, his arms hung at his sides. He had, quite simply, collapsed from exhaustion, like a marathon runner on a hot day. Maxim—at first, apparently, unable to believe his good fortune—began, after a period of ratiocination, to hit after him. He landed one or two fairly good shots, I thought from where I sat. Kearns must have been yelling to Maxim.

And then Robinson, the almost flawless boxer, the epitome of ring grace, swung, wildly and from far back of his shoulder, like a child, missed his man completely, and fell hard on his face. When he got up, Maxim backed him against the ropes and hit him a couple of times. The round ended, and Robinson's seconds half dragged, half carried him to his corner. He couldn't get off the stool at the end of the one-minute interval, and Maxim was declared the winner by a knockout in the fourteenth, because the bell had rung for the beginning of that round.

Sugar Ray, according to the press, was pretty well cut up over his defeat, and in his dressing room, after enough water had been sloshed on him to bring him to, he raved that divine intervention had prevented his victory. This refusal to accept the event is also an old story in the ring, but in the words of John Bee, a rival of Egan, it is "a species of feeling which soon wears out, and dies away, like weak astonishment at a nine days' wonder." On the day after the fight many of the sports writers took the line that Robinson had been beaten by the heat alone, and some of them even sentimentally averred that he had been making one of the most brilliant fights of his life right up to the moment when his legs gave out. They tried to reconcile this with their assertions that Maxim was a hopelessly bad fighter and had made a miserable showing until his unbelievable stroke of luck. It would have required no brilliance on anyone's part to outpoint the Maxim they described. But Goliath never would have been popular anyway.

The heat was the same for both men. This much is sure, though: Whenever a man weighing a hundred and fifty-seven has to pull and haul against a man weighing a hundred and seventy-three, he has to handle sixteen pounds more than his own weight. The other fellow has to handle sixteen pounds less than his. And when you multiply this by the number of seconds the men struggle during thirty-nine minutes of a bout like this, you get a pretty good idea of why they weigh prizefighters. The multiplication is more than arithmetical, of course; a man who boxes four rounds is more than four times as tired as if he had boxed one. I had no idea, from watching the fight, whether Maxim was pacing himself slowly, like Conn McCreary, the jockey who likes to come from behind, or whether he just couldn't get going any faster, like even Arcaro when his horse won't run. But I talked to Kearns a couple of days after the fight, and he left no doubt in my mind about what he wanted me to believe had happened. The nine holes of golf a day, he said, had kept him personally in such condition that he could exercise all the natural alacrity of his perceptions during the conflict. "The heat talk is an alibi and an excuse," he said. "Robinson was nailed good in the belly in the tenth round, and again in the twelfth, and he got a left hook and a right to the head at the end of the thirteenth, when he was on the ropes. If the bell hadn't a rang, he'd be dead. I didn't move Maxim until the twelfth round. I didn't have to. I knew I could win in any round when I got ready. The only reason I shoved Maxim in at all was because I wanted to win with a one-punch knockout. Robinson escaped by luck."

I paused to commit this to memory, and then asked Dr. Kearns, who seemed in high good humor, to what he attributed his victory. "Oh, I don't know," he said modestly. "Anybody who was around those old-time fights we used to have in the hot sun on the Fourth of July knew you had to rate any athalete according to what the heat was. Robinson figured he had any one of fifteen rounds in which to win in. He was going to try for a knockout in every round he fought. But I just told Maxim, 'Just keep this fellow moving, moving. Then he'll have to clinch and hang on.' After that, it just depended how quick I decided to move Maxim. It was up to me to pick the round. Next time I'll knock him out quicker."

"And who do you want next?" I inquired.

"I'd like that Walcott or Marciano," Dr. Kearns replied bravely. "I'll fight anybody in the world."

Since then Robinson has come back, at least as far as being middleweight champion again. After the Maxim fight he retired, and a fellow named Bobo Olson won the title after an elimination tournament among the inept left-overs. Robinson returned to the ring and stopped Mr. Olson in two rounds at

Chicago, which was nice going, and the Cadillacs are back at his door. One fight-writer, reporting the victory, said Olson was a "burned-out hollow shell," which is like merging Pelion and Ossa, or Ford and General Motors, in the cliché business. He must have meant the shell of a broiled lobster after a shore dinner.

Maxim lost his title to a great man, who will be introduced in a later chapter of this book, named Archie Moore, but Dr. Kearns did not say after the bout, "Moore licked me." He said, "Moore licked Maxim."

The Big Fellows Again

NEW CHAMP

BEFORE Marciano fought and beat Louis, Charlie Goldman told me that Rocky was in what he called "an improving phase." "He's still six months—maybe a year—away," Goldman told me. Almost a year passed before Marciano was matched to meet Jersey Joe Walcott for the heavyweight championship. "The great thing about this kid is he's got leverage," Goldman kept saying in the time between. "He takes a good punch and he's got the equalizer." By this last, he meant that Marciano had the ability to equalize—or cancel out with one solid punch —the advantage in points piled up by a more skillful opponent in the rounds preceding equalization.

Marciano knocked Louis out in the eighth round after wearing the older man down. But there was a trace of intellection in the way he finished off the former champion. His right hand had received all the advance publicity, and during the fight he threw it so often, usually missing, that Louis paid less and less attention to the left. Then, in the eighth, Marciano knocked him out with three left hooks and an almost redundant right. The progress of an education, whether that of a candidate for the Presidency or that of a candidate for the heavyweight championship, always interests me. So when I read in a newspaper that Marciano had been matched to fight Jersey Joe Walcott for the title in the Philadelphia Municipal Stadium on the night of September 23, 1952, I went.

A boxer solidly constructed, intelligently directed, and soundly motivated is bound to go a long way. I had not seen Marciano since the Louis bout, but I knew that in the interim he had knocked out several lesser heavyweights to keep his hand in. In the first of these bouts, against Lee Savold, he had seemed to some of the experts to be regressing. I ran into Goldman after that one, and he said, "Yeah, we let him lay off a couple months after Louis, and he went back. He's the kind you got to keep working. We won't make that mistake again." Mr. Goldman added, "After all, they call him crude because he misses a lot of those punches, but it's his style. I could teach him to punch short—across his chest—but to tell the truth it wouldn't be very effective. So let him throw them old Suzi-Qs." In his subsequent fights, Marciano, I noted in the newspapers, finished his chaps off in fast time, winding up with a fellow named Harry Matthews, a clever sort, whom he knocked out in the second round. Matthews' manager, Jack Hurley, had predicted a contrary result, basing his forecast on a mysterious strategy he said he had imparted to his fighter. "Hurley wanted to be a Swengali but the strings broke," Al Weill said to me later.

As soon as I learned that Rocky had been made with Jersey Joe, I went in quest of Weill, to hear how his fighter's education was getting on.

Weill's office then was on the third floor of the Strand Theatre Building, and he had worked out of it for nearly thirty years, retaining it even when he was the Garden matchmaker, as if he knew he would be back there some day. It was impregnated with the smell of the cigars he smokes and decorated with framed photographs and cartoons of boxers he has managed at one time or another. The wide window across the front of the room looked out on Broadway, a street fraught with temptations for fighters to spend money. For this reason, Weill kept his boxers as far from it as possible, usually within earshot of Goldman. He knew he could resist the temptations all right himself. Also, a fighter learns more when sufficiently secluded. Out of sheer boredom, he may listen to some of the pearls of wisdom Goldman casts in his direction, such as "If you're ever knocked down, don't be no hero and jump right up. Take a count," or "Always finish up with a left hook, because that brings you into position to start another series of punches." Goldman frequently voices less technical advice, too, such as "Never play a guy at his own game; nobody makes up a game in order to get beat at it," and "Never buy anything on the street, especially diamonds." Weill now has an office in the Hotel Lexington, on the more fashionable East Side, as befits the manager of the heavyweight champion of the world, but it doesn't smell right yet. It takes a heap of smoking to give a hotel suite the atmosphere of a humidor.

On the morning of my call, I found Weill looking out the window and smoking a cigar while waiting for, he at once in-

when he is outside the ring, has a pleasant asymmetrical grin on it. It is the grin of a shy fellow happy to be recognized, at last, as a member of the gang in good standing. His speech doesn't fit the type caster's idea of what a prizefighter's should be; he speaks with that southern New England accent in which the "a" in "far" is sounded as New Yorkers sound the "a" in "hat," and the "a" in "half" is sounded as we sound the "a" in "far." Grammatical constructions are more carefully worked out there than in most parts of the country, and Marciano (whose name in this dialect becomes "Masiano," with two short "a"s) sometimes sounds more like former Senator Lodge than like one of his own professional colleagues working on the New York–Chicago–California axis. He is, in fact, as much of an exotic, in his way, as was Luis Angel Firpo, the man in the celluloid collar. Weill, mindful of the pitfalls of Broadway, is anxious to keep him that way. Marciano goes back to Brockton after every fight. Each expedition into the outside world has for him the charm of an overnight trip with the Brockton High School football team, on which he once played center, and, like the team, he is accompanied by hundreds of home-town rooters. When I asked him, for lack of a more original question, how he felt, he replied, with an accent I remembered from my days on the Providence *Journal*, "Peufict." He is not exactly gabby.

The workout in the hangar that day was not spectacular. Marciano boxed two rounds with a colored light heavyweight from California named Tommy Harrison, a fast, shifty fellow who kept stabbing and going away while Rocky slid along after him. It was logical to expect evasive action from Walcott, a cel-ebrated cutie who had never, as far as anyone could remember, made a standup fight with any opponent. Against Rocky, who was notoriously slow afoot, the champion might be expected to circle and move in and out even more than usual. But the test was inconclusive, since Harrison, who weighed a hundred and seventy and was in his early twenties, was certainly faster than Walcott, who was by his own admission thirty-eight and weighed nearly two hundred. And Rocky would have fifteen rounds, not two, in which to catch up with the old fellow.

Then Marciano did two rounds with Keene Simmons, a colored heavyweight every bit as big and rugged as Walcott, and much younger. Simmons had once given Marciano a pretty good fight in public. His imitation of Walcott was good —he would throw quick sneak punches, some of them right-hand leads, and slide away. When he didn't slide away, he clinched. He even did the kind of jig-step shuffle Walcott uses to disconcert his opponents, although there is no particular reason it should. Marciano, I noticed, wasn't throwing as many long, looping punches as he threw the previous year. He couldn't afford to be caught off balance by a sharpshooter like Walcott, who could move in fast on any mistake. But I remembered what Goldman had said about Rocky's ineffectiveness with short punches. I wondered what he would use against Walcott in place of "them Suzi-Qs." His boxing had improved vastly—from terrible to mediocre—but I couldn't imagine him outpointing Walcott. He would have to keep crowding—pushing him around until the spring went out of the old man's legs and arms and it was safe to revert to the Suzi-Q.

After the workout, a fellow drove Rocky back to the house —a distance of a few hundred yards—and Goldman and Columbo and I followed on foot. When we got there, the boxer was already lying on a bed in a second-floor room, warmly covered to keep him sweating. "This is the best part of boxing," he said. Goldman talked to him about old fighters; I noticed that, unlike veterans, who want to talk about anything but boxing, Marciano was intensely interested. He seemed to be trying to build up background for the position he felt he had been called to. When Marciano went downstairs for his shower, Columbo told me how they had come out of the Army together when they were both twenty-two, and how Rocky had started boxing in amateur tournaments in New England. "He was crude, but there was one move he would wait for the other fellow to make, and when he made it, Rocky would swing and knock him out," Columbo said. "He must have knocked out a hundred. Half the time he would hit them on top of the head. One time he broke his right thumb on a bird with a hard head, and they laid him off at the shoe factory where he worked. So he knew he would have to make up his mind—either give up boxing or the shoe factory. By that time, Weill had seen him, and he offered to carry him along for the first year or so if he would turn pro, until he started to earn real money. So he turned."

The fighter came back and Goldman rubbed him down. I asked him again how he felt, and he said, "Peufict."

Rocky's father, addressed as Pop by the trainers and sparring partners, ate supper with us, at five-thirty. His name is Pietro— or, affectionately, Pietrone—Marchegiano. ("Marciano" is a contraction adopted for the convenience of fight announcers.) He is a small, thin man, gravely polite, with a heavy Italian accent and a most un-Italian reserve. From the day of his arrival in America until recently, he cobbled shoes in his own one-man shop in Brockton. Only in his large, strong hands does he resemble his son. While we ate—a good-sized steak apiece, with bread and butter, string beans, and potatoes—the telephone rang almost continuously. Most of the callers were well-wishers in Massachusetts and Rhode Island, asking for blocks of good tickets to sell to friends. One said the Mayor of Brockton was coming to the fight and was bringing the Governor of Massachusetts and Adlai Stevenson as his guests.

While waiting for an automobile to pick me up—the plane had long since gone back to New York with the photographers and their undeveloped plates—I stood on the lawn for a moment with Charlie Goldman. "The shoe factory that laid him off sends him a new pair of boxing shoes before every bout," he said. "They done it for his last ten bouts, and every pair has his name inside. Everybody rides with a winner." The little man looked up at me and said, "You know, there are two kinds of friends—the ones who are with you when you are winning and the ones who stick when you are losing. I prefer the second kind. But you got to take advantage of the others while you got them. Because they won't be with you long."

A fortnight later I boarded the five-o'clock train to Philadelphia at Pennsylvania Station with a twenty-five-dollar ticket in my wallet and a small but good pair of binoculars in my pocket. There were six Brocktonians across the aisle from me. They made no secret of their civic identity. Florid men with small, merry eyes, all in clothes slightly tight for them—probably, like trees, they added a circumferential ring each year—they might have been either union officials or downtown businessmen, types hard to distinguish between in their part of the world. They were organizing a two-dollar pool among themselves on which round Rocky would win in. One, addressed by the others as Mac, caused indignation, which I judged to be not entirely feigned, by saying that for his two dollars he would take Walcott by decision.

"Then we'll be laying you five to one," one of his townsmen said.

"You don't think Walcott has a chance, do you?" Mac asked. "I'm doing you a favor." I could see he had raised a doubt in their minds, and at the same moment he saw he was losing popularity. "I just said it for laughs," he added lamely.

But their journey to Philadelphia had been spoiled. Mac had opened up a possibility they had shoved resolutely into the back of their minds. In forty-two fights, Rocky had never even been knocked from his feet.

On arrival, I took a subway to the center of town and walked about for a while, looking for Lew Tendler's restaurant. Tendler is an old Philadelphia fighter who has remained a Philadelphia idol because, I think, he embodies the city's sense of being eternally put upon. He once had Benny Leonard beaten when Leonard was lightweight champion; Leonard was on the floor but got up before "ten," and it was a no-decision bout. I thought I knew where Lew's restaurant was, and wouldn't ask anybody the way. I soon got tired of walking, though, and ate in a place called Mike Banana's. A minute after I had finished and left, I found Tendler's, but I saw I couldn't have eaten there anyway. I couldn't even have got as far as the bar, it was so packed. The sidewalk on Broad Street in front of the restaurant was jammed right out to the curb, and gentlemen with embossed ears were struggling to keep from being pushed under taxicabs. Everybody (I use the word in its Ward McAllister sense) who goes to Philadelphia for a fight meets at Tendler's and tries to put the lug on somebody for a free ticket. On the night of the twenty-third of September, the people with the free tickets had apparently sold them to scalpers. Some, in their enthusiasm, had even sold their own seats, and were now looking for friends to put the lug on. It was a scene of great confusion. Joe Walcott, in a car preceded by a police escort, passed by on his way to the fight. The main bout would not go on until ten-thirty, but he wanted to get there in plenty of time. Walcott is from Camden, New Jersey, across the river from Philadelphia, and the crowd in the street cheered. I had thought I could put the lug on somebody for a ride to the stadium, but the only acquaintance I met who had a car had to wait for somebody who had promised him a ticket. I was lucky to get a seat in a taxi.

The Municipal Stadium, situated in a kind of Gobi Desert at the end of all transportation lines, can, it is said, seat a hundred thousand. The crowd of forty thousand in attendance filled one end of the oval grandstand and, of course, a great carpet of "ringside" seats on the grass inside the running track. I found that my fifteen inches of concrete in the stand afforded a good view, with the aid of binoculars, except for a minute segment of the ring that was masked by one of a number of tall steel masts that were disposed around its circumference. I suppose they had something to do with the public-address system, since they all had capitals of entwined horns, like morning-glories. However, I had an aisle seat, and by stretching far out, like a runner with a lead off base, I could take this obstacle in enfilade in a matter of seconds. The preliminaries gave me a chance to adjust my lenses and perfect my moves to the right and the left of the post. They had no other interest for me.

When the main-bout fighters entered the ring with their factions, I saw that Weill had decided to act as Marciano's chief second. He had four subordinates, of whom the smallest, and consequently the hardest to see, was Goldman. One of Weill's strongest points of resemblance to Napoleon—or, for that matter, to Mr. Pickwick—is what he calls his "built." He worked from a standing but bending position directly in front of his seated fighter and facing him. As Marciano was in the corner diagonally across from my perch, my only memory of what happened there between rounds centers on the seat of my old friend's white flannel pants. All I could see of Walcott was the back of his head.

The fight was, as you probably read, one of the stubbornest matches ever fought by heavyweights. When all the lights except those over the ring went out and the bout started, I began to be aware there had been a mistake, and I soon recognized what it was. Walcott, a great, earthen-hued man, mature but sprightly, has a cylindrical torso and a smaller cylinder of a head rising directly out of it. He weighed a hundred and ninety-six pounds, twelve more than Rocky. And the mistake was that he was not imitating Keene Simmons' imitation of him. Instead he was walking forward, hitting at Marciano and moving him back. In just about a minute he landed a beautiful left hook to the jaw, and the hope of Brockton went down on his left side. Walcott started to walk away, assuming, I suppose, that anything human so hit would take the longest permissible count—nine seconds. But Rocky jumped up at three. (This was the only thing Marciano did all night that Goldman complained of after the fight.) Walcott turned, unable to believe his good fortune, but didn't get back to him soon enough. The way Marciano came up made me think the hope of Brockton was out of his head. I learned afterward that what had made him bounce was a combination of indignation and inexperience. The remainder of the round was not reassuring to the Brockton rooters, and when the old fellow continued to batter Charlie's pupil in the second, I was reminded of the remark of a trotting-horse man I know, made in similar circumstances: "The cow got loose and killed the butcher."

There was a colored man to my right, entirely surrounded by whites. I could hear him yelling, and what he was yelling hardly sounded sensible—though, come to think of it, it may have been. "Don't get mad, Joe!" he was hollering. "*Please* don't get mad!" But Walcott continued to act mad, walking right out to meet Marciano in the third. Half a minute later it was Marciano who was shaking the champion, knocking him back with body blows and punches that did not land clean on the jaw but hit him on the side or the back of his bobbing head. The old fellow gave way slowly, hitting all the time, not breaking away and circling, as he had in other fights. Pierce Egan would have called his tactic "milling in retreat." The match now seemed to be following the script more closely. Rocky was slowing him down. The old man would go in a couple more rounds. If he started running he might last a little longer. The young fellow kept pounding in the fourth and fifth. At the end of several rounds they continued after the bell, and Marciano usually got in the last punch. At the end of the fifth I couldn't understand how Walcott stood up.

Then, in the sixth, there was blood all over Walcott's white trunks and Marciano's matted chest. It didn't show on Marciano's trunks, which were black, or Walcott's torso, which was nearly so. Walcott, I could see with the glasses, had a cut over his left eye. Marciano was bleeding, too, but from an unlikely place—the top of his head. You could figure how head and eye must have come together. Marciano, an inch or so shorter than Walcott, accentuated the difference by fighting out of a crouch; his game was to get his head in against the bigger man's chest, where Walcott couldn't hit it, and then punch up, and when he stepped back out of one clinch, his head had come up hard. This accident, the crowd thought, would hasten Walcott's end. In the seventh, though, it was, unaccountably, Marciano who began to flounder. He wavered and almost pawed the air, although he had not been hit by any one particular big punch. He seemed to be coming unstuck, and in the eighth it was the same. Walcott's seconds had closed his cut after the sixth round, using one of those mysterious astringent solutions trainers treasure. And Marciano's corner had closed the wound on his scalp. But now Marciano's right eye had been cut by a punch. (Late that night, or early next morning, at a party given by a man called Jimmy Tomato, who had won a good bet on Marciano, I was told by Weill and Goldman that Rocky, nestling his brow against Walcott's chest early in the seventh round, had got a liquid in both eyes that blinded him. They did not know whether it was some of the astringent solution, dripping from the cut above Walcott's eye, or just liniment, well spiked with capsicum, which Walcott's seconds had sloshed on their man as a form of chemical warfare. "He fought four rounds that he couldn't see the guy," Weill said. I thought this an exaggeration, because in the ninth Marciano had recaptured the lead, which was pretty good going for a blind man.)

In nine rounds the lead changed hands three times—Walcott to Marciano in the third round, Marciano to Walcott in the seventh, Walcott to Marciano in the ninth. You don't see many fights like that. In the tenth, which was the hardest-fought round of all, Marciano stayed on top. But somehow the calculations had gone awry; the old fellow looked further from collapse now than he had six rounds earlier. It might go

to a decision, after all. I thought with pity of my Brocktonians
on the train. If it was close, I felt, Walcott would get the decision. It is traditional not to take a championship away on a
close one, and Philadelphia was virtually his home.

Then Walcott, as if bolstered by the certainty that he could
last, came out for the eleventh and had his best round of the
fight, except for the opener, when he had floored Rocky. It was
the fourth switch in the plot. In the twelfth, he looked not
only more effective but stronger than the challenger. Up to
then I had had the feeling that if Marciano did land flush on
the jaw, he could take the champion with one punch. Now his
arms and legs seemed a trifle rubbery. He was swinging wildly,
and missing by absurd margins. At the end of the twelfth, Walcott was well ahead and looked stronger than ever.

In the thirteenth the fighters disappeared momentarily from
my view behind that steel mast. They were doing nothing particularly exciting. Walcott was giving ground slowly, backing
toward the ropes, as he had done repeatedly. Whenever he
reached the ropes, he would start a rally; it was a habitual tactic of his. Marciano was following—hopelessly, it seemed. He
had to keep moving in, because if he stayed away Walcott, who
had a much longer reach, could hit him without return. I
wasn't as quick going into my own crouch with the binoculars
as I had been in the early rounds; perhaps I was feeling slightly
rubbery myself. Then I heard one of those immeasurable shouts
that follow a ball over the fence in a World Series. And I could
see Walcott's legs protruding to the right of the mast. The fellow next to me, who thought he had seen what happened,
yelled, "I can't believe it! He knocked him cold with a left
hook. Who said he could hit with a left?" This miserable crea-
ture, who by sheer luck had been looking when I wasn't, invited my contempt, and I shouted back, "Who said he couldn't?
He knocked Louis crazy with lefts! He belted Matthews cold
with a left!" Actually, as I learned later, Rocky had knocked
Walcott out with a right that traveled at most twelve inches,
straight across his chest to the champion's jaw. The guy next
to me hadn't seen the punch at all; Marciano had had his back
toward our side of the ring. But Marciano had grazed Walcott
with a left hook as the champion fell, already dead to the
world. "He trun it for insurance," a fellow who had been in his

corner told me later. The fan could be excused, of course. The sports writer of the Philadelphia *Inquirer*, sitting at ringside, wrote that Rocky had hit Joe with a "roundhouse right, swung from his hip and his heart." The punch was the antithesis of a roundhouse; it was a model of pugilistic concision. The newsreel film of the fight shows that both men started right leads for the head at the same moment. Walcott, the sharp, fast puncher, figured to get there first in such an exchange. But Marciano hit sharper, faster, and, according to old-timers, about as hard as anybody ever hit anybody. Walcott, the film shows, flowed down like flour out of a chute. He didn't seem to have a bone in his body. And so, after old Jersey Joe had piled up a lead by fighting the way he wasn't supposed to, Rocky knocked him out with the kind of punch he wasn't supposed to know how to use. "In other words," Charlie Goldman said to me at Jimmy Tomato's party in the Hotel Warwick after the fight, "he equalized." Mr. Tomato, whose real name few of his acquaintances remember, is a businessman and patron of the arts who has been known to bet on Marciano. From the scale of the party it was safe to conclude his investment had been more than nominal.

When the referee, a Pennsylvanian named Charlie Daggert, had counted Walcott out—a hollow formality—all the ringside-seat holders from Brockton, Swansea, Taunton, New Bedford, Attleboro, Seekonk, Pawtucket, Woonsocket, East Providence, Providence, and even Hopkinton, Hope Valley, and Wakefield climbed over the shoulders of the sports writers, kicked them under the typewriter benches, stamped on their typewriters, and got up into the ring to shake hands with Rocky. It seemed that they might pluck his arms off like petals from a daisy, but somehow he escaped and came shooting through the crowd, propelled by the long line of admirers pushing along behind him. A group of police cleared the way and the fellows from his corner locked arms behind him to keep the jubilious from pawing him over. He disappeared under the stand almost at a dead run.

As for Walcott, I can't even remember seeing him leave.

LONG TODDLE, SHORT FIGHT

The spectator who goes twice to a play he likes is pretty sure of getting what he pays for on his second visit, especially if the cast is unchanged. If it is a three-act melodrama when he first sees it, he can be reasonably sure it won't have turned into a bit from the repertory of burlesque the next time he drops in. This is not true of the form of entertainment that the Herodotus of the London prize ring denominated the Sweet Science. For one thing, a prizefight contains within itself the seeds of its own abrupt termination, a possibility of which the members of the fancy are well aware but which they push back into a neutral corner of their unconscious when they set out for the scene of a return match. For another, it is always possible that there has occurred, subsequent or consequent to the first encounter, a change in the emotional relationship of the two principals.

This last was the case with the pair of combats between Tom Oliver the Gardener, the hero and champion of Westminster, weighing a hundred and seventy-five pounds, and Ned Painter, whom the great Egan describes as "a customer not easily to be served," weighing a hundred and eighty. Their first fight, at Shepperton-Range, near London, on May 17, 1814, moved Egan to rapture. Writing of the third round of their battle, he exclaimed, "Such a complete determined *milling* round is not to be met with in the Annals of Pugilism, and there was more execution done in it than in many fights of an hour's length. It was enough to *finish* any two men. By a correct stop-watch, it continued FOUR MINUTES AND A HALF AND TWELVE SECONDS!" (A round by the rules of those days lasted until one man or the other went down, and half a minute separated the rounds. A round now lasts three minutes.) In the eighth round, "Painter was quite done up, and Oliver finished the contest in prime style." As evidence of their sincerity, the historian noted, "they were both *punished* in the extreme, and Painter was quite blind, and his nose beat flat upon his face. Oliver's body was terribly beaten, his head much disfigured, and one of his eyes nearly closed."

At the end of six years—things went more slowly then—the men were rematched to fight in the village of North Walsham, twenty miles from Norwich, Painter's home town. Egan says that the contest "excited an unusual degree of interest in the sporting circles; and numerous parties, for a week previous to the fight, left the Metropolis daily, to be in time to witness this combat." After a mere fifty-five minutes of rather dull milling —"the *punishment* that both the combatants received," Egan skeptically records, "was so truly light for such heavy men that they were up at an early hour the next morning to breakfast" —Painter floored Oliver with "a tremendous blow upon his temple." Half a minute elapsed—he would have had a minute at the end of one of our rounds—and Oliver didn't come to. He passed the time sitting on his second's knee, the custom in an age when stools were not permitted within the ropes. But when Painter had been proclaimed the victor, Oliver "rose (as from a trance) from his second's knee, and going up to Painter said, '*I am ready to fight.*' 'No,' said Painter, '*I have won the battle.*'" And that was that. "It is true," says Egan, concluding his account of this ambiguous ending, "that many ill-natured remarks have been made upon the termination of this battle; nay more, that it was positively a X between the combatants. It is the duty of an impartial writer to mention this circumstance; indeed, he could not pass it over. But it is equally his duty to observe that nothing like PROOF has been offered to substantiate it was a X. . . . At all events, no man possesses a higher character for a deserving well-behaved man in society, whether in Lancashire, London, or Norwich, than NED PAINTER." By "a X," Egan meant "a cross." A "cross fight" was a bout in which one of the combatants had agreed to lose. A "double cross" was one in which the man who had agreed to lose didn't.

To complete the discomfiture of the fight fans who had traveled all the way from London to see this mystery—and who had mostly bet on Oliver—it was followed by a great downpour of rain. "The hedges were now resorted to, and hundreds sought for shelter even under the slightest sprig or a bush; and those who *scampered* off to North Walsham had not a dry thread about them long before they reached it. The *daffy* and *eau de vie* [gin and brandy] were tossed off like milk, to put the *toddlers* (who were as exhausted as drowning rats) in *spirits.*" By "*toddlers*" Egan meant pedestrians. "In short, the road beggared all description—it was a fine *finish* to the fight—and the *Bonifaces* never had such liberal customers before, that they might very fairly exclaim, 'It is an ill wind that blows nobody good.' "

The annals of the modern ring are not lacking in anecdotes about fights that ended prematurely. Most of them follow the same pattern. Arrived at the ringside, the man who has traveled great distances to get there lowers his head for some trivial reason. He looks up and the fight is over. Practically every ancient who ever told me that he was at the fight between Bob Fitzsimmons and Peter Maher, in 1896, across the Mexican border from Langtry, Texas, was lighting a cigar when Fitzsimmons knocked Maher out in a minute and thirty-five seconds. A Norwegian ship broker on whose integrity banks have ventured millions in pounds has assured me that after a trip from Oslo just to view the fight at the London National Sporting Club, in 1913, between Georges Carpentier and Bombardier Wells, he was verifying the number of his seat when Carpentier dispatched Wells in the first round. My friend Colonel Stingo, who in 1908 took the then heavyweight champion, Tommy Burns, a Canadian, to Dublin to fight an Irishman named Jem Roche on St. Patrick's Day, is exceptional in that he had his eyes fixed on the principals when Burns leveled Roche in a minute and twenty-eight seconds. "He dazed him with a grazing left to the chin," the Colonel told me, "and then, while Roche stood there as if frozen, he struck him a blow that would have felled an ox. He fell like an avalanche instead, and I could see on Honest Tom's face a puzzled expression that denoted, 'How long has this been going on?' Only blind chauvinism could have induced those people to think Roche had a chance."

I should have had in mind all these gloomy precedents before I took the plane to Chicago to see the return bout between Rocky Marciano and Jersey Joe Walcott. No unpleasant thoughts marred my journey, however. In the words of Colonel Stingo, I "let disinclination limit the horizon of my anticipation"—always a dangerous procedure. I like going to fights.

When I awoke in my Chicago hotel room on the morning of May fifteenth, the date set for the championship match, the sun was already high in the heavens, although, since my chamber gave upon a court, I was not immediately aware of it. I was reminded of where I was by the sound of the police whistles, which in that city sound like sea gulls' cries, except that they have two syllables. Instantly remembering the occasion of my presence, I arose and called room service for two three-and-a-half-minute eggs—they arrived hard-boiled—and the newspapers, from which I learned that the combatants were to weigh in at noon at the Chicago Stadium, the scene of the fight that night. I had been of the opinion, ever since the previous fall, that Marciano probably would repeat his victory, because he was of an age when a conscientious fighter is still capable of improvement, while Jersey Joe was of an age when most boxers have long retired from competition and the best any fighter can hope for is a slow rate of deterioration. But the lapse of eight months since their Philadelphia go seemed hardly enough to make the return bout one-sided. Marciano would have the advantage of added confidence, but he had always had plenty of that. Since one thing I couldn't find in the papers was an advertisement saying where tickets were on sale in downtown Chicago, I decided to go out to the Stadium for the weigh-in and buy my ticket there. I could have bought one in the hotel lobby, I suppose, but the prices were quite steep enough without paying a commission. And, besides, it was a lovely morning and I had nothing else to do.

Most of the sports writers in the papers seemed to take roughly my view of the probabilities, although they phrased them more elegantly than I would have thought possible before I boarded the plane. "Bald on top but smart inside, old Jersey Joe Walcott is razor sharp and ready to shear boxing's gold-crusted heavyweight crown off champion Rocky Marciano's proud, unbowed head tonight at the Chicago Stadium," a figure-of-speech man named Wendell Smith, of the Chicago *American*, began his piece. "The most amazing, durable antique in the museum of mayhem, the thirty-nine-year-old challenger intends to cut the rugged champion down with his slashing, powerful tools of destruction as quickly as possible and become the first fighter in history to regain the heavyweight title. Tradition says he can't do it. Seven others have had the same opportunity and failed. The gods of chance are against him, too. They've made old Joe the 3–1 underdog. They're heaping their affections and blessings on the young man—the bull-like king of clout from Brockton, Mass., who strikes with the terrifying might of Thor and lightning suddenness of Ajax. The experts, too, believe Walcott is about to be sacrificed upon the altar of futility." This was just about the way I saw things.

But another fellow on the same paper took a diametrically opposite view of the situation. His name was Tom Duggan, and he spoke with an authority I had previously associated with only one other name in Chicago, that of Colonel Robert Rutherford McCormick. "Jersey Joe Walcott is going to win back his heavyweight boxing title out at Octopus Palace tonight," Mr. Duggan said, without qualification of any variety. "I think he'll win it by a knockout within seven or eight rounds. . . . The press-rows for this fight will be filled to the scuppers with self-appointed experts on the manly-art-of-self-defense. You would do well to remember that most of these guys are familiar with fighting only to the extent of their wives taking a belt at them for sneaking in past curfew time with a load on, garnished with lipstick on their collars. . . . I have never been in favor of running benefits for anyone, but, in Marciano's case, I would like to make an exception. After this fight, I think we should all pass the hat for him. . . . He not only is giving his title away but forcing Walcott to take most of the money along with it. . . . I'm astonished at the odds the professional gamblers are maintaining on the fight." This put a different light on the match. As I started for the street, I wondered how Al Weill, ordinarily a shrewd fellow, had allowed himself to be caught in such a trap.

The Stadium, which, as I knew, is not a stadium but a large shed, is about two and a half miles from the center of the Loop, but I had a full hour to spare, so I walked out along West Madison Street, past the Morrison Hotel, which was headquarters for Marciano and the visiting press; past the Civic Opera House, with a sign on it proclaiming the imminent arrival of Louis Armstrong and Benny Goodman; across the Madison Street drawbridge over the piddling Chicago River; past the soot-blackened Northwestern Railroad station; and then along the most readable thoroughfare in America, the part of West Madison that has the flophouses and the signs— "Second Shot Your Favorite Whiskey 1/2 Price," "Mamie's

amount taken in at the gate, along with thirty per cent of the 3-D rights. The champion was to have thirty per cent of the gate, thirty per cent of the television and radio take, and thirty per cent of the 3-D rights.

I bought a thirty-dollar ticket, which entitled me to a seat in Row F of the first balcony, overlooking the ring. This essential preliminary disposed of, I took a streetcar back to the Loop and walked to Mike Fritzel's restaurant, where I had a date with a friend. Fritzel's is a kind of Chicago Lindy's, and as I went in I met a New York comedian named Jack E. Leonard, who told me he was playing at the Chez Paree, a Chicago night club. Leonard was sad because he wouldn't be able to see the fight. The headliner at the Chez was Tony Martin, the singer, and Martin also was a fight fan. Somebody had to do the early show, and Martin had pulled rank on Leonard, who would therefore miss the fight. He is probably still laughing.

The fellow I was lunching with told me a bit about Mr. Duggan. Duggan, he said, had had a sports program on N.B.C. television, in the course of which he had needled the identical ownership of the Stadium and the International Boxing Club, and had predicted that the fight would never be held in Chicago. N.B.C. had dropped him—yielding to outside pressure, according to Duggan; nothing of the sort, according to N.B.C.—and the Hearst *American* had picked him up as a sports columnist. He had christened the Stadium Octopus Palace because it is the home of the boxing octopus that controls professional fighting all over the country. He was already famous even to the outmost suburbs as a champion of free speech, a fearless iconoclast, and an exponent of the locally popular thesis that everybody in the world is trying to put one over on Chicago. I ventured the thought that Duggan's prestige might be damaged by the fact that the fight was going to be held in Chicago after all, but my informant said I didn't understand how the Chicago mind works. "They'll say the fight *wouldn't* have been held here unless Duggan had blown the whistle," he said. "It'll make him bigger."

After lunch, I went back to my hotel to rest. This is always a good idea before a big fight, because you are going to have to battle crowds going in, you can never find a taxi coming out, and you often have to toddle home without benefit of daffy unless you are willing to battle more crowds to get to a bar. The spectators sometimes take as much *punishment* as the fighters, and on this particular evening, as it turned out, we were to take considerably more.

At eight o'clock I took a taxi to within a third of a mile of the Stadium, and dismounted when my vehicle could no longer advance. The first preliminary bout was to go on at eight-thirty, as it usually does in big shows, but the main bout was to begin at nine instead of ten, because it would have to be on the air at ten in the Eastern time zone. One result was that the hordes of people who customarily stream in between nine and ten were for once hurrying to get to their seats early. To extract the maximum amount of fun from this situation, the Stadium management had decided to admit ticket holders at my gate only in single file, like candidates for a crap game, each one squeezing by the belly of a large special policeman, who half blocked the interstice through which we were eventually admitted. Now and again, he would stop the whole line to permit the egress of someone governed by a premonition; I can think of no other reason why so many people would want to come away from a fight before it started. When we had finally been allowed to proceed to the point where a guard was waiting to snatch our tickets, we were turned onto the first of six flights of concrete stairs and at length run down a ramp to our seats. The layout had evidently been designed by the same chap who built the stockyards, but fight followers have been a hardy lot since Egan's day. I arrived at my perch, which was as exiguous as a racing saddle but harder, full of that exhilaration that always precedes what old Pierce would call a contest of heroes. I could not sit back. The customers adjoining me had already arrived, and both of them overlapped their thirty dollars' worth of space by several inches. But by adopting a forward crouch, which I modeled after my recollection of how Eddie Arcaro rides a finish, I was able to maintain a kind of equilibrium and enjoy a good view of the ring. While we were thus wedged in, venders of binoculars and hot dogs, who merely block your vision as they walk down the aisles in other cities, walked over our feet and crawled over our laps.

I took to reading the biographical notes in the official program. The one I liked best was about Walcott. It began, "If public support was the decisive yardstick in Jersey Joe Walcott's bid to become the first boxer ever to regain the heavyweight championship, the popular 39-year-old Negro would be assured of the distinction when he encounters Rocky Marciano tonight. Few fighters have won the heart of the public as has this wholesome, deeply religious father of six children."

There were two preliminaries before the main bout, and they fitted into the half hour with several minutes to spare, since both ended in quick knockouts. Neither presented any semblance of competition. Then Walcott and Marciano and their handlers came into the ring, hurriedly. Television time schedules have taken the old dragging dignity from the overture to a championship match. There were a number of garbled introductions of visiting prize-ring celebrities, the announcer never seeming to know the name of the fighter in the ring but always announcing the name of a fellow who had just left or one who was still making his way up through the crowd. Of the former champions introduced, only Tony Zale, the middleweight, got a big hand. Ezzard Charles, who lost the heavyweight title to Walcott, and Jim Braddock, who lost it to Joe Louis, were present too, but the old champions with the greatest names, Jack Dempsey and Joe Louis, weren't.

Then the ring was cleared. As the hour hand of the big clock on the balcony facing us neared nine, the principals went to the center of the ring to hear the referee make his brief speech, and then returned to their corners. Marciano jumped up and down in his—he was trying to warm up for a fast start—and Walcott sat quiet, waiting for the bell. In a moment, the fight started. Because all these anterior events had been crammed into a half hour, it was still very early in the evening. There were great blocks of empty seats at the ends of the vast shed, both on the arena floor (euphemistically called ringside), and in the mezzanine and first balcony. All the empties were fifty- and thirty-dollar seats. In retrospect, the judgment of the people who didn't buy them seems excellent. (Alter the bout, the I.B.C. announced that the fight had been attended by around sixteen thousand people, of whom a bare thirteen thousand were paid admissions. It drew a gross gate of $331,795, which included the federal and state taxes on each ticket.)

Marciano had a whole swarm of handlers in his corner— Weill; Charlie Goldman, described in the program as "an elf from Brooklyn with a broken nose"; Columbo; Freddie Brown, a fight handler good at stopping cuts; and Marty Weill. When they left the ring and the bell rang, the champion looked lonely. He sought the company of the only other human up there with him, Walcott. But the wholesome, religious father of six children was not in a sociable mood.

A small colored man far off to my left cried encouragingly, "Come on, Satchel!"—a reference to Satchel Paige, a big-league-baseball pitcher, who was even older than Walcott but sometimes came through in tight spots. There was no great conviction in his voice, and none at all in the way Walcott handled himself. In September, I had seen Walcott walk out and beat Marciano to the punch. But this time he neither punched nor skipped; he just backed away. And Marciano, never a fast starter, couldn't think of much to do but walk after him. When he got close, Walcott grabbed his arms. It appeared to be the kind of fight we could all settle down to. The excitement, if any, would not come until the late rounds. The pace was so slow that I looked a couple of times at the big clock that measures off each three-minute round. Walcott flicked a couple of left jabs at Marciano as he retreated, but he was going away so fast that they fell short. Marciano missed a couple of right swings that were so clumsy I thought they were feints, designed to draw some counteraction. If so, they failed. Then, while the two men were groping about in Marciano's corner, the champion with his back toward our side of the house, I saw Rocky throw a high left hook, and Walcott hit the floor. I learned afterward that Marciano had thrown a rising right to the jaw immediately after the left, but I couldn't see it land from where I sat. So I simply assumed Jersey Joe had been knocked down with a left hook.

It wasn't a crashing knockdown, the kind that leaves the recipient limp, like a wet hat, or jerky, like a new-caught flatfish. This appeared to be a sit-down-and-think-it-over knockdown, such as you might see in any barroom on a night of full moon.

Jersey Joe must have begun the process of ratiocination right away. But the conclusion at which he was arriving was not instantly apparent. Like the drowning men in stories, he may have been reviewing his whole life, with a long pause on what had happened to him in Philadelphia. The dramatic significance of the fleeting seconds was lost upon the crowd, because everybody present, with the possible exception of Mr. Walcott himself, took it for granted that he would get up within ten seconds. And maybe he thought so, too, for a while, but if he did, he dismissed the thought. Sprawled on the canvas floor covering, his right arm hooked over the middle strand of the ropes, he waited for the referee to count ten, and arose. Even then it was not clear to us in the balcony that the fight was over. Unable to hear the count, we assumed that he had risen on nine. But when the referee, a slight man named Frank Sikora, spread his arms wide to indicate that all was ended, Walcott walked calmly over to the ropes on our side of the ring, evincing a commendable independence of public opinion. If he had maintained this attitude, I would have admired him. The spectators were resentful, and their resentment was based on the suspicion that he had not been hit hard enough. This is a decision every man must make for himself, and of all the sixteen thousand persons under the big shed, Walcott was in the best position to make it. But as he heard the boos, he changed his mind. He mimed outrage, batting his gloved hands together and stamping like a wrestler. Wrestling is classed as a species of exhibition by the New York State Athletic Commission, and the acting is part of the show. Jersey Joe made it plain that he had not been knocked out at all. The crowd, with a forlorn hope that the fight might be resumed—after all, it had got precious little action for its money—increased its booing, but it was now booing *for* Walcott. Jersey Joe had stolen the scene from the man who had knocked him out. (And yet no man possesses a higher character for a deserving well-behaved man than ROCKY MARCIANO.) The whole fight had lasted two minutes and twenty-five seconds. The Kentucky Derby this year lasted two minutes and two seconds, and nobody cried, "Stop thief!" But fight fans are accustomed to more protracted pleasures.

*

Like the toddlers of North Walsham long ago, I made for the nearest lushing crib to restore my spirits. Going down the concrete stairs of the Stadium in front of me were three men, one of whom shouted, with what sounded like immense satisfaction, "This will kill boxing in Chicago!" One of his companions said indignantly, "I thought they were going to work it the opposite, so there'd be a bigger gate next time." It was evident he felt hurt because "they" had disappointed him. The third said, with a bitter laugh, "Write Duggan a letter."

In the Stadium Tavern, the closest dispensary of daffy and *eau de vie*, I caught one of the bartenders tying on his apron. "I sneaked off to watch the fight and I had to run like hell to get back here for the rush," he said. I had one Scotch, which I tossed off like milk, and headed for a streetcar. There were plenty of cars, because a good part of the crowd had remained behind to watch the rest of the minor bouts on the card, hoping to salvage a few nickels' worth of amusement. I found myself sitting next to a knowing drunk, a pale old man who was the shade and shape of a fat, soft clam. "Waidle you read the papers tomorrow," he said exultantly. "Duggan'll burn up the paper."

"What for?" I asked. "Duggan said Walcott would kill him."

The old drunk winked and snorted. "But he knew sumpm was up, dint he?" he said. "He couldn't write all 'at stuff if it wasn't true, could he? They'd soom."

A man with a flashlight gun and camera—a newspaper photographer who had been at ringside—was telling anybody who cared to listen what had really happened. "It was a right uppercut that did it," he said. "He tried to get up, but he couldn't make it in time." (The moving pictures of the count, however, show that Walcott didn't start until it was all over.) "Read Duggan!" the photographer yelled as he swung off the car. I think he meant to be funny, but a stout man sitting with a woman shouted a protest after him, "But Duggan predicted—"

I stopped briefly in the lobby of the Morrison, where friends and admirers of Marciano were giving a party to celebrate his victory. A couple of the kids in green jackets were standing there when Al Columbo breezed in, straight from the Stadium. "He didn't butt him this time!" Mr. Columbo yelled.

I decided I didn't want to go to a party, and went on to my hotel and bed.

Next morning, I bought an armful of Chicago newspapers at the airport and read them on the plane going home. The first columnist I turned to, naturally, was Duggan, and he was as omniscient as if he had been right. "If the Illinois Boxing Commission has the guts God gave a lazy white dog," he began, "they'll hold up those purses till they get a look at the films of last night's fiasco to determine what knocked out Jersey Joe Walcott. . . . Out here in a hick town like Chicago, I guess anything can happen. Everybody knew the fight had no business here in the first place. It was a natural for New York in June. But say what you want about New York, you can be sure they wouldn't stand for the exhibition we put up with last night." I have never seen the man, but I make him no worse than even money to wind up as mayor. He had proved that, like everything else that goes wrong in Chicago, it was New York's fault. We had planted that fight on them like a road company of *The Student Prince*.

CHARLES I

In my study I have a print by Thomas Rowlandson of a milling match between Tom Cribb, the champion of England, and Tom Molineaux, an American Negro, at Thistleton Gap, in the County of Rutland, on September 28, 1811. This was a return fight; Molineaux had very nearly won the first, and Pierce Egan, the Froissart of the London prize ring, wrote concerning the second match, "It is supposed that near 20,000 persons witnessed this tremendous *mill*"—which, since it was an illegal event and all the customers had to dodge the constabulary to get there, denoted a high intensity of interest. Cribb won the fight at Thistleton, and there were bonfires in the streets when the news reached London. Rowlandson's picture was turned out with journalistic speed to profit by the public excitement. Cribb has just landed a mighty right to the jaw, stepping in with the punch in smashing style, and

Molineaux is falling. There have been few artists like Rowland-son for catching action without arresting it. But the detail I recall first when I think of the picture is the face of Bill Rich-mond, one of Molineaux's seconds and also an American Negro, as he sees his man go. He is following Molineaux down with his eyes, bending as the challenger falls, and his face is desolate.

I sat in the fourth row behind Ezzard Charles' corner when he fought Rocky Marciano at the Yankee Stadium on the night of June 17, 1954, and what I shall remember about that fight longer than anything else, I imagine, is also a face. It was not Charles'—although that became a memorable sight in itself as the fight wore on—but the face of a plump, light-colored man named Jimmy Brown. Charles, like Molineaux long ago, is a Negro, and Brown, like Richmond in my print, was a second. There is much about Marciano, with his square torso, short, heavily muscled arms, and granite jaw, that recalls the Cribb of the picture, and he is as appallingly discouraging to fight. Each time Charles came back to his corner after a round, his seconds took the same positions about him, to save time and eliminate confusion. Brown was in front of him, facing the crowd as he bent over the seated fighter. Before Charles went out for the first round, Brown pressed his hand reassuringly on the chal-lenger's left knee, and when Charles came back to his corner after drawing first blood from Marciano's nose, there was a look on Brown's wide, oval ecru face that said, "There, now, it wasn't so bad after all, was it?" It seemed to me—and, as it turned out, to both judges, the referee, and all the press—that Charles had outboxed the champion in that first round, as well as bloodied him. As Charles got past the second and third rounds, still leading, Brown's face relaxed, and after the fourth, when Charles opened a dangerous cut on the champion's left eyelid with a right, Brown grinned over the fighter's shoulder like one who saw before him a rosy future as the traveling companion of a world's champion. (I have no doubt that he had a good bet on, too, and the gamblers' odds on Marciano were 18 to 5.)

It was another Brown—Freddie Brown, the white "cut man" in Marciano's corner—who was worrying then. He used adren-alin to check the bleeding, a mineral jelly over the surface, and a quick-hardening plastic shield over all, but he knew a good punch would wreck his repair job; the cut was two inches long and an inch deep. "With a cut like that, you got to be nervous," he said afterward. "A quarter of an inch further in and it would of run like a faucet."

Marciano kept on swinging in the fifth; as the bell rang, Charles hit Marciano one punch, and the champion came back with a couple of determined swings, both launched well after the round ended. Charles looked very gay, to use an Eganism, when he came back to his corner; you could see that he felt he had the champion flustered. And there was always the cut to work on, a deep and promising little gold mine. There is a difference of a couple of hundred thousand dollars between the champion's and the challenger's share of a million-dollar gate. If Charles could work his vein properly, the return match would be sure to draw that. Jimmy Brown was still looking happy, as a man looks at Belmont when he sees his horse in good position and running easy. Both corners covered their men with robes of Turkish toweling between rounds; the night was cool, and a sweating fighter stiffens if the chill gets to him. Standing behind Charles and with his back toward me was one of his managers, a big Greek, who kept a hand on the fighter's left shoulder, as if to steady him, while he talked into his right ear. Charles is a temperamental boxer and sometimes has emotional blocks. Ray Arcel, a trainer who handled him in an exasperating failure, once said, "He is like a good horse which won't run for you." Arcel is severe and decisive, like a teacher in a Hebrew school. This time, Charles' corner was trying sweetness. The Greek's hand was soft and manicured, and a large diamond on his middle finger refracted the ring lights. As the ten-second klaxon warned the seconds to leave the ring, the hand gently urged the fighter forward, taking the robe as Charles stepped out of it.

Then came the sixth round. It was a round in which Marciano's apparently clumsy blows began to rock the challenger. The blow that really started Charles' decline, though, was a short, jarring left hook to the jaw that wasn't clumsy at all. One of the things that make Marciano a disconcerting opponent for a good boxer like Charles is that even his awkwardness is inconsistent; every now and then he does something highly skilled. Abruptly, Charles began to go slack, like every other fighter I have seen after Marciano's punches have begun to tell; they have a cumulative effect that asserts itself suddenly. When Charles sat down in his corner after that round, Jimmy Brown's face was grave, and the Greek's fingers beat a brief tattoo on the toweled shoulder before they remembered that they were there to soothe. I thought the finish would come in another round or two. It had been quite as good a fight as I had expected. I had not taken too seriously the reports from the training camp that this was a "new Charles," determined to do or die, but even if I had, I shouldn't have thought he was strong enough to take Marciano's blows for fifteen rounds. The spring came back into his legs after the bad round, though, and he went out and fought savagely, never avoiding the issue, in the seventh and eighth. This was the Indian summer of Charles' fight.

The bounce and snap had left him for good now, but what the sports writers had said about his determination was true. As for his endurance, it was unbelievable. His face—rather narrow, with a high, curved nose—changed in shape to a squatty rectangle as we watched; it was as though he had run into a nest of wild bees or fallen victim to instantaneous mumps. He moved, hung on, twisted his body, rolled his head on his columnar neck, which was now a cable between aching body and addling brain. He broke to his right, away from Marciano's swinging rights, but he didn't run. He even punched—straight but without power. He was doubtless admonished in his corner that he still had a chance to win on points if he could just keep going. But between rounds his toweling was getting soaked with blood, and Jimmy Brown's face—concerned, anxious, horrified, and finally despairing—was like Bill Richmond's in my picture. Some of the newspaper experts (trying, it seemed to me, to make too much of a good thing) said the next day that it was still a close fight in the late rounds, because the men were almost even in rounds won; Charles had taken five of the first six, by some counts. If he had rallied and won the last three, they said, he could have earned the decision. But there was no possible chance that he could rally, since the strength was out of him; there was a much better chance that he would collapse. That he didn't is great credit to his game-ness, but if, like Cribb and Molineaux at Thistleton Gap, he and Marciano had been fighting to a finish, Marciano must have finished him off. After the announcer, Johnny Addie, who looks like a younger and plumper Billy Rose, had read the de-cisions of the two judges and of the referee, Ruby Goldstein, all agreeing on Marciano, Jimmy Brown achieved a histrionic triumph. He managed to look indignant.

It had been a hard fight but not great, in my opinion, because there were none of the sudden changes of fortune that mark a great one, as in the first Walcott-Marciano match. This time, Charles' success in the early rounds was expected, since he is a faster, better boxer than Marciano. The cut he inflicted on Marciano in the fourth round gave the champion's backers, including his vociferous fellow townsmen from Brockton, only temporary anxiety. The one true surprise was the loser's capac-ity for punishment. As Egan said of the Thistleton Gap mill, "The hardiest frame could not resist the blows of the *Cham-pion*; and it is astonishing the Moor stood them so long."

It was a mighty crowd—paid admissions 47,585, and, count-ing deadheads like me, a total attendance of more than fifty thousand. There were fifteen hundred occupants of working-press seats alone, including a major general in uniform and Joe Louis. As is usual at big outdoor fights nowadays, platoons of young hooligans from the bleachers stormed down on the field in successive waves, to take over better seats than they had paid for. Legitimate ticket-holders who arrived late managed as best they could. In some cases, with the aid of ushers and special cops, they expropriated the squatters. These, however, made it a point of pride always to move forward instead of back, so that by the time the star bout began, they were standing all over the poor devils who had paid forty dollars for the use of a folding chair. The goal of the game, apparently, is to get to lit-eral ringside, with the press photographers. This proved im-possible during the big fight, but after it was over and the photographers went away, a swarm of adenoidal lummoxes came clambering over reporters' shoulders to get to ringside for the four-round bout that always follows a main event. "We're in fifty-dollar seat zat last!" one boy brayed as he dropped down by my side after a hurdle race over the backs of chairs. I was happy to note that the lagniappe bout ended with a sudden knockout while he was still breathing hard.

After the fights, I walked up to 167th Street to get a seat on a subway train before it reached the Stadium, which is at 161st. Several hundred other people seemed to have thought of the same stratagem, and it worked for all of us; the squares who got on at the Stadium found no seats and had to stand all the way downtown. They may well have been the seat-stormers. This provided a happy ending to the excursion.

CHARLES II

Pierce Egan, the Sire de Joinville of the London prize ring, characterized the immortal Tom Cribb as "placid, condescending, and obliging." "If not possessing the volubility of an orator," Egan wrote, "the CHAMPION, in company, is facetious, and endeavours to render himself pleasant and sociable to those around him, with a modest and unassuming deportment." Dr. J. L. Moreno, described by the Associated Press as a noted psychiatrist and author, visited the training camps of Ezzard Charles and Rocky Marciano before their recent fight at Yankee Stadium, and gave Marciano even higher marks. Marciano, like Cribb, is a forthright, outgoing type in the ring. "He has poise, charm, sensitivity, imagination, a remarkably retentive memory, and a rugged handsomeness," Dr. Moreno wrote in the second article of a series of three sent out to all A.P. member papers, but, unfortunately, not used by any of the New York dailies. I was wised to Dr. Moreno by a member of the staff of the Newark *Evening News*, which had better editorial judgment. "He is friendly, warm, winning, and appeals to women, especially when he smiles," the analysis continued. Dr. Moreno is not a woman, but he took his wife along to the training camps to supply feminine reactions. "Marciano has presence of mind," he wrote. "That is a most important thing —a most decisive factor in the ring. Absence of mind is most devastating to a pugilist. Marciano has the ability to concentrate immediately on the crisis. . . . He is not calculable. His concentration is intense. . . . Unlike Ezzard Charles, Marciano has no inhibitions. Charles is the dreamer type."

I suppose the A.P. sent a psychiatrist to the two camps because when Marciano and Charles fought for the first time, Charles, who was in the estimation of the fancy a timid fighter, stood up to the champion for fifteen rounds, thus confounding the lay analysts who hang out in Stillman's gymnasium. It was the general opinion of these unlicensed practitioners that Charles' brave fight had been a temporary flight from reality, or fugue, which was not to be expected in the return match. "That kind of beating stays with a guy" was how one of them explained his prognosis.

The schema, or main idea, of the training-camp series was that Dr. Moreno would visit Charles and analyze him in his first article, visit and analyze Rocky in his second, and then, in his third article, for release on the day set for the fight—Wednesday, September 15, 1954,—tell who was going to win. But for an old psychiatric buff like me, that line about inhibitions blew the gaff. I knew a day in advance that Dr. Moreno was touting Marciano. It was not a highly negotiable piece of information, because so was everybody else.

From the first article, however, I could see that Charles was really the one who interested Dr. Moreno. He probably wished he had had time to work on those inhibitions before they calcified. An inhibition is a challenge to a psychiatrist, like a leaky faucet to an amateur plumber, and, seeing Charles on the rubbing table, Dr. Moreno must have felt tempted to get out his notebook and have a try, even at the eleventh hour. "Charles is a dreamer," he wrote. "In his dreams, he is a mighty, invincible fighter, who sweeps all before him in a reckless, savage, destructive fashion. In the ring, however, he loses the spontaneity he has in his dreams." It was almost a miracle, he went on, that Charles had got as far as he had in the ring. "Can a 'miracle' happen again?" he asked himself point-blank. "Yes," he answered himself. "If Charles can wipe out his inhibitions in a frenzy—for just thirty seconds—if he is as spontaneous as he is in his dreams, he might knock out Marciano or anyone else. He would be irresistible. He would be like a tiger fighting for his mate. If the dream man can loose the tiger from within him, then Marciano had better watch out. There are several mental blocks, however, that have held back the tiger. Charles is an intelligent, cultured, well-mannered, sensitive person. He intuitively resents that part of his primitiveness which he loathes at times in other fighters. . . . Because of this conflict, Charles is neither a primitive slugger nor is he a classic boxer. [Here the Doctor may have stumbled on the explanation of switch hitters in baseball.] He is part puncher and part boxer."

The Wednesday piece appeared in the Newark *Evening News* under a headline contributed by a member of the staff who is probably an extrovert, like Rocky:

DOC PICKS ROCK
BY A KNOCKOUT

"After making a psychological study of Rocky Marciano and Ezzard Charles, and weighing all the factors involved," Dr. Moreno said, "I pick Marciano to knock out Charles tonight in one of the middle rounds, probably the seventh or eighth. Charles, a split personality, has to fight himself as well as the champion. . . . Ezzard, the way I see it, has but one way to win—a slim one at best. If he can rid himself of his emotional blocks in a frenzy, if he should cut or hurt Rocky and then turn loose the 'tiger' of his dream personality, then he could stop Marciano. But he must knock out Marciano to win. As the rounds go by, the possibility of a wild onslaught by Charles decreases. . . . Psychologically, the chances for this to happen are extremely small. Rocky is positive and supremely confident. He has no fears to hold him back. He is of one piece."

After that, the Doctor began to sound like an old A.P. sports writer. "I expect to see them both start slowly tonight," he wrote, "with Marciano permitting Charles to meet him halfway. Charles will be cautious. He will retreat and counter. In the second or third round, Marciano, who generally warms up slowly, will suddenly take over the offensive and begin to crowd Ezzard. In the fourth and fifth, Charles may break loose once or twice in short spurts, but something will hold him back from letting loose to the fullest. Then Marciano, supremely assured and confident, will assert himself. He will move in with short, punishing blows and begin to wear Ezzard down. Rocky may knock Charles down in the seventh and finish him in the eighth round."

Having read Dr. Moreno day by day, I felt *au courant* with the psychological situation when I walked over to Madison Square Garden at noon on Wednesday to see Charles and Marciano weigh in. In addition, I had acquired a pretty good notion of the somatic prospects from a piece in *Sports Illustrated* by Dr. Paul Peck, an anatomist, who had furnished drawings of both men stripped of their skins, like the charts in patent-medicine shows. Dr. Peck had labeled all the muscles from the zygomaticus to the gastrocnemius. (The zygomaticus is the muscle under the cheekbone; the gastrocnemius is way down in the leg.) "If the fight were held in a swimming pool, with both boxers treading water," Dr. Peck said, "Rocky wouldn't be able to hit very hard. Charles would." As it was already raining when I set out for the Garden, I thought this might be worth pasting in my chart book.

The weighing-in before a heavyweight fight is completely irrelevant, since the men do not have to make any stipulated weight. It provides photographs and new leads for the afternoon newspapers, however, and has a social function. Admission is by card (police) or badge (a tin ear), giving all visiting journalists and milling coves, active or retired, a place of rendezvous where they can exchange autobiographical notes since the last fight. It also gives you a chance to see who is in town. This time, I noticed, none of the British boxing writers who had covered the June fight were present—an indication that the London editors didn't think Charles would loose that tiger. The weighing of Marciano and Charles seemed particularly unimportant because it was plain from the weather that there would not be any fight in a New York ball park that night. Marciano weighed a hundred and eighty-six and a half and Charles a hundred and ninety-two and a half—a gain of seven pounds over his ring weight in June; with my new psychiatric orientation, I attributed it to compulsive eating, caused by anxiety. The champion looked as placid, pleasant, and unassuming as ever. His placidity, it appeared, had in the course of years spread to all his faction. Al Weill, who in the past had been a fuming, worrying kind of man, wore a fat, paternal smile.

Charlie Goldman, who three years before, when Marciano was training for Louis, had acted like a tutor trying to teach a boy the whole of mathematics in time for a college-entrance examination three days away, now had the relaxed air of a professor emeritus. Charles, taller than Marciano and of a fashionable charcoal shade, looked about as excited as a man waiting for a subway train. The weather forecast for the next day, Thursday, was unfavorable, and it occurred to me that a forty-eight-hour prolongation of the dreaming period might accentuate Charles' internal conflict, if Dr. Moreno was right in diagnosing one. I voiced this thought to Mr. Jimmy Brooks, a Harlem *boulevardier* and associate of pugilists, who chanced to be at my elbow, and he agreed. "It does not pay for a fighter to be too intellectual, brainy—you get my meaning?" Mr. Brooks said. "They get to laying awake and thinking too much about their physical body—what might happen to it, you know?"

Mr. Brooks did not attend the second weighing-in, which was held on Friday, September seventeenth, when the weather cleared. Neither did any of the other people who had come to the first one for purely social reasons, since nothing to talk about had developed in the intervening two days. Just the newspapermen and photographers showed up, to repeat the routine of the first ponderation. This time Marciano weighed a hundred and eighty-seven, a gain of an inconsiderable half pound (he had been doing enough gymnasium work to hold his edge), and Charles registered no change. After the weighing-in I had lunch in Gilhuly's saloon, near the Garden, with a fellow who said that a movie producer had wanted to bet him thirteen hundred dollars to two hundred on Marciano, but that he didn't see how Charles could win.

"Oh, I don't know," I said. "He is a very complex MacTavish. If he could wipe out his inhibitions for just thirty seconds, he would be like a tiger fighting for his mate."

"I never thought of that," the fellow said. "Excuse me while I give this wise guy a bang on the telephone." He came back and said he had taken the bet.

Late that evening, I made my way up to Yankee Stadium by subway. The curtain for the main bout was to be fashionably late—at eleven o'clock. It was practically a supper show. This was in order to avoid a conflict with a baseball game at the Polo Grounds, half a mile away, where the Giants were playing the Phillies; the game had begun at eight-fifteen. On Wednesday night, when the fight had been rained out, the Giants had not been scheduled to play. The late hour of the match made for a long, straggling evening, with the crowd assembling slowly.

The preliminaries were, if possible, worse than usual, to judge from the three I saw. The six principals in these three had all appeared on the Marciano-Charles card in June, and none had improved over the summer. This time, I sat behind the corner that was to be Marciano's—in June, I had landed behind Charles'—and during the next-to-last preliminary Al Weill sat down in front of me, to root for a moderately belligerent hundred-and-seventy-five-pound man in whom he had a proprietary interest. "Stop hoppin'!" Mr. Weill would shout at him, and then "Stick, stick!" meaning stick him with your left hand. "I know what they should do," he said when he happened to turn around and see me, "and it hurts me when they don't do it." Since Mr. Weill's champion was going to defend the world's heavyweight title within twenty minutes, his preoccupation with such a trivial performance indicated to me that he wasn't worried.

The notorious dreariness of the preliminaries at championship fights is due to a feudal arrangement whereby the managers of the main-bout fighters get berths for all their fighter's stablemates and sparring partners on the preliminary card. The promoter fills in the remaining spots with the cheapest boxers obtainable. Sparring partners are endowed with habitual consideration and forbearance, and they find it hard to change character. A kind of guild fellowship holds them together, and they pepper each other's elbows with merry abandon, grunting with pleasure like hippopotamuses in a beer vat. Mr. Weill left to change into the form-fitting garments he wears in the ring as Marciano's second, and his man floundered through to a decision.

After the last preliminary Whitey Bimstein, the trainer of one of the participants in it and an old friend of mine, came down from the ring, his face wearing an expression designed to apprise the world that there had been a miscarriage of justice; the officials had called it a draw. Whitey's fighter, less experienced in mimesis, looked as if he were glad to have escaped with his life.

Now Marciano's faction began pushing its way toward the ring along a narrow path left between the massed undertaker's chairs on which the International Boxing Club mounts its patrons. Cops and bodyguards cleared a passage, and then the fighter appeared, wrapped in a blue bathrobe with a cowl over his head. He would have four men in his corner: Columbo, Weill, Goldman, and Freddie Brown. Weill would handle the stretegy, Goldman the tactics, and Brown the surgery. Columbo was there just because he couldn't live if he weren't. Goldman and Brown are old fighters—small men with mashed noses and quick eyes. Colombo is young, and in his white sweater he looked like a college cheerleader. Weill is onion-shaped and authoritative; Marciano, when I first met him, used to call him "Mr. Weill." The demeanor of all was confident, but what was especially impressive was Marciano's back when he had seated himself on the stool in his corner. It looked as wide and as immovable as a blue wall. There was a brief fashion show as Floyd Patterson, a young light heavy who is coming along, and Sugar Ray Robinson were introduced from the ring. They were both sharp, but I thought Robinson, in yellow haberdashery and a black suit, had it.

At about six minutes after eleven the fight began, and it was lucky I had Dr. Moreno's scenario with me, because from where I sat I missed occasional fractions of action. In the June fight, Charles had moved out faster than Marciano, stepping in and hitting him away with rights. This time, however, he was acting like an intelligent, cultured, well-mannered, sensitive person, gracefully poised. I could but recollect the time-honored Egan's description of Richard Humphries, the Gentleman Boxer, in his second contest with Dan Mendoza, at Stilton in 1789. "Humphries had lost that commanding style which was so prominent in his last attack; and he seemed to labor under an impression that he had a superior to encounter with; he did not maintain his ground with his usual confidence, but suffered his opponent to drive him, and even, upon some occasions, there was a sort of shrinking from the blows of his adversary." Marciano, forcing the fighting, missed most of his punches, but he came back to his corner grinning. For him it was a pretty good start.

Meanwhile a considerably more acrimonious round had been contested behind Marciano's corner, where his seconds, coming down from the ring, had found themselves with nothing to sit on but photographers and account executives' friends. Columbo, hopping up and down with excitement—he was probably the only person in the Stadium so affected by that round—had aroused the wrath of an Athletic Commission inspector sitting to my right. The inspector ordered Columbo to sit down, so that he, the inspector, could see; if Columbo had sat down, *he* couldn't have seen. The function of a second during action is, as Freddie Brown says, "to see if he can see anything" worthy of communication to his principal between rounds. Weill said to the inspector, "He got a right." Columbo started to say something, too, but Weill cuffed him on the back of his head. Marciano, blissfully unaware of all this ill-feeling, was the calmest man in the corner when he returned at the bell.

In the second round—to my amazement and, apparently, to Charles'—the champion began to use a straight left, jabbing to the face with jolting force and then crossing a right, exactly as they teach in boxing school. ("He is not calculable," as Dr. Moreno had it.) For years little Charlie Goldman had refrained from trying to teach Rocky anything so fancy, on the ground that it might "spoil his natural leverage." It was as fancy as A B C. Goldman must finally have decided it was safe. Before Charles could react to this treacherous attack of orthodoxy, Rocky landed a right to his zygomaticus, and he went sprawling down, forgetting to tread water, until he hit the bottom of the pool. The referee, Al Berl, counted to two, and Charles got up. ("In the second or third round, Marciano . . . will suddenly take over the offensive.") When Charles went down, I had a feeling he would stay there, like Walcott in Chicago, but he didn't. He had too much self-respect. However, he didn't take the count of nine, to which he was entitled, and this may have been because he didn't trust his self-respect that far. Marciano, moving in and swinging, the fancy stuff forgotten, appeared to have him headed for a quick knockout, but Ezzard rid himself of his emotional blocks for a fleeting second. He hit

Marciano two dazzling left hooks, which, coming from a fighter apparently on his way out, gave the only intimation, however brief, that this could be a good fight.

Between the second and third rounds, inhibitions coagulated in Charles. In the third round, Marciano plodded after him, sometimes landing and more often missing, but Charles' intuitive resentment of violence had set in like ice on a pond. Understanding the psychiatric problem, Marciano concentrated intensely. Meanwhile the battle of Al Columbo continued, but the inspector couldn't get at him without climbing over Jack E. Leonard, the fat comic who missed the fight at Chicago. In the fourth round, my score card recalls, Marciano feinted a left beautifully and followed with a right hard enough to rearrange anybody's emotional pattern, and, sure enough, in the fifth Charles displayed a pinch of spontaneity. I thought he won the round, but I also thought it was academic.

The sixth round brought Freddie Brown his chance to operate. Marciano, for all his toughness, cuts easily, and in the first Charles fight got a long cut over the left eye. In this fight, Charles' right elbow collided with the champion's nose, inflicting a deep, wide cut along its bridge. Marciano came back to his corner with an embarrassed grin, as if asking to be excused for putting his seconds to so much trouble. Brown, after stopping the chink with a quick-setting plastic called Thromboplastin, topped it off with a generous handful of Vaseline, which made the champion look as though he were wearing a Halloween false nose. Even this, however, failed to unleash the tiger in Charles. Once, when Marciano stuck out that rudimentary jab again, Charles countered with a fine right to the champion's head, delivered over Marciano's arm. But this was an intellectual rather than an emotional response. He wasn't weak—once he grabbed Marciano by the back of the neck and spun him—and he wasn't entirely unresentful; when Marciano hit him after the bell, he hit back. I remember thinking, as I looked at him in his corner after the sixth round, that he was strong and unmarked, but I was perfectly sure he would be knocked out, and sure that he was sure of the same thing.

The two men wallowed through the seventh round— Marciano slugging away, the Vaseline dissolving in blood, and Charles intuitively resenting the primitiveness of it all. Early in the eighth, Marciano caught Charles with a series of blows that knocked him down. He took four this time, rose, and reeled away, with Rocky hitting at him. The knockdown was on the side of the ring to the left of the champion's corner; Charles staggered across the base of the triangle, and there Rocky hit him again, this time using a sweeping left, like a man swinging a brush hook. Charles went down, and Marciano nailed him with a right as he fell. We were all on our feet, watching, and at four Charles pulled himself up to one knee. It was the better part of discretion to take the count of nine, and I expected him to rise when Al Berl, counting in his ear, reached that numeral. Instead, he stayed a second more—a very long second—and Berl said "Ten." Maybe he had just forgotten to get up; as Dr. Moreno says, absence of mind is most devastating to a pugilist. The Doc, as a matter of fact, had called the round.

After the fight I shared a cab with a friend, and we rode all the way down to the Artists' & Writers' Restaurant, formerly Club, on 40th Street, and had a beer. On the way, he said that Marciano was a travesty of a champion, but that it was all right; one great champion was all a man could expect in a lifetime, and he had seen Joe Louis at his best. I said that Marciano was so good, in his peculiar way, that there should be a law against allowing him to fight return bouts. "He takes it out of them," I said. Neither of us was happy. It just hadn't been a good fight.

It wasn't until I dropped in at Stillman's the next day that I got a reasonable non-Freudian explanation of Charles' conduct. Freddie Brown and Whitey Bimstein were sweating a number of their future champions between calls on what is known in Stillman's as the long-distant phone. Hurricane Tommy Jackson, the colored heavyweight with the double uppercut, was hitting the big bag on the gymnasium balcony. Mr. Jackson, a temperamental young man while on a winning streak, had been a model pupil ever since the unfortunate termination of a bout with a Cuban heavyweight named Nino Valdes; the referee stopped the bout and awarded it to Valdes at a moment when, according to Hurricane, "that man was so tired he was staggling."

Mr. Bimstein was, as usual, bemoaning the effect of television on the development of new talent. At nine-tenths of the boxing shows nowadays, he said, you might as well be fighting in a telephone booth, and only the feature bout is televised. Fighters in the preliminaries, therefore, labor practically in private, unremarked even though they perform prodigies.

I congratulated Mr. Brown on his job on Marciano's nose, which had at least remained attached to the champion's face, and he said it had been an unusual kind of injury but one that had not found him unprepared. When I propounded Dr. Moreno's theory of the caged tiger within Charles' breast, it met with polite skepticism from Mr. Brown. "Why did he fight that way, then?" I asked.

Mr. Brown looked at me with placid, obliging condescension. "He fought the way he fought because Marciano fought the way *he* fought," he said. "Charles come in in a good mental condition, and he started right in to execute—biff!" Mr. Brown here took the stance of a confident, standup boxer. "But Rocky is coming in." Mr. Brown here came in, and I stepped back. "It is very hard to think when you are getting your brains knocked out," Mr. Brown said. "So Charles withdraws back to consider the situation." Mr. Brown withdrew. "That puts him further from a position where he can execute. Meanwhile, Marciano is still coming in. He is cruel. Charles hits him a good right to the jaw, and Rocky hits him with a left hook *and* a right. First thing Charles knows, he is grabbing, and then he is just trying to hang on. Why? He don't know why. It is not like football," he said, kindly, like one trying to convey truth to little children. "Rocky never gives you the ball."

Other Fronts

THE BOY FROM SOUTH MAIN STREET

Like every American city, the capital of Rhode Island cherishes its sporting celebrities. When I worked as a reporter on the Providence *Journal* and *Evening Bulletin*, in the late twenties, one of the walking monuments of the town was Norman Taber, a trustee of Brown University, who soon after graduating from Brown had set the world's record for running a mile—4:12⅗, I think it was. Another monument—and quite a nice one, too—was Glenna Collett, the National Women's Amateur golf champion. Brown's Iron Men had just gone undefeated through the football season of 1926, and the Providence Steamrollers won the professional-football championship in 1927. Gus Sonnenberg, the Steamrollers' star tackle, was flattening visiting wrestlers every week in the Arcadia Ballroom by a tactic of almost miraculous simplicity—butting them in the belly. But the town had never produced a world's boxing champion. It was not for lack of aspirants; the weekly amateur tournaments at the Arcadia dance hall drew crowded entry lists. Nor was it for lack of scheming—there were more old fighters around than you could shake a towel at, all saturated with good counsel and looking for a likely young ear to pour it into. There was a shining example of ringcraft to observe; a Providence boxer called Young Montreal—his real name was Maurice Billingkoff —who had boxed six world's bantamweight champions and, according to local belief, beaten them all. He had beaten three even according to the record book, and had boxed no-decision bouts with two of the others; unfortunately, he had never been able to beat one of these fellows at the precise moment when the fellow was holding the championship. When I saw Young Montreal, he was past his prime but still a most elusive, exasperating man in the ring. He was bald and had red freckles and pipestem arms, and in his pugilistic old age I saw him make a fool of Bud Taylor, one of the hardest punchers who ever lived. I was on the city side then, but I could usually get a free ticket from the sports department. It has always seemed to me

a historic injustice that Monty never held a title—something
like Gustave Flaubert's failure to receive an invitation from the
Académie Française. While I was in Providence, a young featherweight named Ernie Mandell showed promise—he was a good,
graceful boxer—but he got knocked out by a Filipino from
Cleveland, and never did much after that. And in the twenty-
six years that have passed since my departure from that tran-
quil town, it had produced perhaps a dozen fair fighters, but
never one who went all the way to a title.

A few years ago a cellist and former journalistic confrere of
mine who still lives in Providence told me there was a lightweight boxer up there who showed signs of real virtuosity. The
boy's name, he said, was George Araujo, and since the cellist
himself had been an amateur boxer of some technical capacity
when I first knew him, I made a mental note of it. From time
to time after that, I saw wire-service stories about Araujo on
the sports pages, their progressively increasing prominence re-
flecting his rise, and then I read that he was matched to fight
the lightweight champion, Jimmy Carter, for the world's title,
at one hundred and thirty-five pounds, in Madison Square
Garden on the night of June 12, 1953.

The lightweight class has been in a decline in recent years,
for reasons as hard to explain as the non-appearance of bluefish
in seasons when they are expected. My learned friend Whitey
Bimstein has attributed the extinction of good "bantyweights"
—hundred-and-eighteen-pound professionals—to the increase
in the stature of the human race, but there are still great numbers of young men visible who stand, say, five feet six or seven
inches and can do a hundred and thirty-five, which is the lightweight limit. Because of the drop in the class's prestige, the
Carter-Araujo bout did not get the publicity buildup that a
lightweight-championship fight would have got in the days of
Benny Leonard, who drew nearly half a million dollars into the
Yankee Stadium when he fought Lew Tendler there in 1923, or
even in the late thirties, when there were lightweights around
like Tony Canzoneri, Barney Ross, Henry Armstrong, and Lou
Ambers. Instead of writing about the match for weeks in ad-
vance, as they did when the middleweights Randy Turpin and
Ray Robinson were to fight here in 1951, and when Rocky
Marciano was to fight Jersey Joe Walcott, the sports colum-

nists waited until the last week, and then gave it one story apiece, unless they happened to be too immersed in baseball to bother about it at all.

Because of this matter-of-fact approach to the fight, I suppose, Araujo's managers didn't take him to a training camp in the country before the fateful evening. They must have reasoned that for a young fighter who has been performing as often as he had—he was twenty-two and had had fifty-two bouts in the previous four years or so—a training camp is simply a touch of swank. Besides, it costs money. So a week before the fight they checked him into the Capitol Hotel, a gaunt hostelry on Eighth Avenue, one block north of the Garden and three south of Stillman's Gymnasium. He worked out at Stillman's and did his running in Central Park. Carter, more of a traditionalist, trained in Summit, New Jersey.

Araujo had been a year short of birth when I left Providence, so when I climbed the stairs to Stillman's to see him work out three days before the fight, I had, perhaps, a fuller sense of the civic responsibility that weighed on his shoulders than he had himself. As I entered Stillman's the challenger was in the ring sparring with a slightly heavier boy. I could see that he moved gracefully, and with almost too much confidence, in and out under the other fellow's leads, bouncing around as if his legs were so good he enjoyed using them. Naturally, with the fight so near, he wasn't trying to kill his partner. A fight manager watching the workout said that he thought the boy held his hands too low—he was open for a right counter over his left. But I couldn't believe that this was inadvertent; I decided it must be his style, and that he relied on speed of eye and head to slip such punches. It is the style of fools and perfectionists. It is also the kind of thing that only a fellow very sure of himself can do, and to be so sure of himself he must have boxed thousands of rounds. This was in fact the case with Araujo, I learned from his senior manager, Frankie Travis, a sallow, heavyset man with grizzled, wavy hair and a jutting chin, to whom I was introduced at ringside. "I saw George the first day he came up to the Catholic Youth Organization, on South Main Street, and put the gloves on," Travis said. "He was eight years old, and he had so much stuff I said, 'That kid is going to be a champion.' I've been training him ever since."

(When Travis said "South Main Street," he brought to my mind a water-front street with flophouses and tattooing shops in eighteenth-century buildings and Portuguese barbershops and ship chandlers' stores whose windows were decorated with prints of Lisbon before the earthquake. It is on the east side of the Providence River, which is the head of navigation on Narragansett Bay, but no great ships have come that far up the bay for a long time. The great ships of Providence's great days as a seaport drew precious little water.) "But he didn't start seriously until he was thirteen," Travis added, as if to discourage the thought that there had been anything unusual about Araujo's childhood. In Providence, Travis is sometimes a Portuguese name—an Anglicization of Tavares. But the manager said his name had originally been Italian—Trevisano. Araujo's other manager was Sammy Richman, a younger, Broadway sort of fellow, who came into the act six months before the Garden fight. He was the outside man, or negotiator, while Travis was the professional instructor and personal counselor. Out-of-town managers, like out-of-town lawyers who have cases in New York, frequently retain metropolitan associates. "He's a good boy," Richman told me, "and I don't think he will get too pent up—you know, freeze."

The boy came down from the ring. He is a mahogany lad, the son of one of those sailors from the Portuguese Cape Verde Islands, off the west coast of Africa, whom New Englanders sometimes call Bravas, although Brava is the name of only one island in the group. Long ago, Cape Verdeans used to make up a good portion of the crews of New England whalers, and hundreds of the islanders still come to New England in sailing schooners every spring to work through the summer on construction jobs and on farms. In the fall the schooners sail back to the islands—thirty-five to fifty days away—occasionally leaving behind a part of their spring complements and carrying home other Cape Verdeans, some of them naturalized American citizens. A lot of Cape Verdeans born in the islands are American citizens because their parents were born or naturalized in New England. They are the last sailing-ship people anywhere, I suppose, who aren't yachtsmen and don't use auxiliary engines; even the Finns have given up their grain fleet. Araujo's father, one of the island-born Americans, sailed to the United States and stayed. He worked on the Providence docks, married, and begot seventeen children, and now there is nothing in his son's voice that isn't New England, and nothing in his manner that isn't Hope High School.

Travis introduced the fighter to me and then sent him along to the locker room for his rub. Araujo, I noticed, had a small head, a compact torso, and big, round arms and calves—not much reach but a good build for endurance and mobility. "He's my baby," Travis said. I asked him if he had had other good boys, and he said, "I once had a fellow named Ernie Mandell that was pretty good, but he got flattened by a Filipino. And I had a boy named Al Mancini that beat Sixto Escobar, but it was over the weight." I figured he had been waiting at least thirty years for a big fighter.

We went into the locker room and sat around the rubbing table in the cubicle rented for Araujo. While the boy sat on the table, we talked about Providence. A fighter I remembered named Eddie Holmes was now a bus driver, I learned, and another named Billy Lynch, who once gave Lou Ambers a lot of trouble until he got a bad cut—the old Providence luck—was a lieutenant in the Fire Department. Young Montreal had a job with a labor union. Knockout Billy Ryan had dropped dead, and old Joe Murphy, the retired bare-knuckle fighter who ran the bottling works on Transit Street, had finally passed on. With the money earned from his fifty-two fights, Araujo had moved his family away from South Main Street and into a neighborhood with less character but more sanitation.

Neither Travis nor George professed any worry about Carter. "He can box, but he's not an expert boxer. And he can fight, but he's not an expert fighter," Travis said. "And he's better than a fair hitter. But he's not getting any younger." This was about what I had heard elsewhere concerning the champion. George had little to say, but he appeared to feel the *Wunderkind*'s contempt for the plodding mediocrity. Travis said he had lost just two decisions in fifty-two fights and had been knocked down only once in his life. That had happened four years before, and he had got up to win easily. I asked George who had taught him most of his stuff, and he said Travis had taught him everything. "I would practice moves with another fighter, and he would coach me," he said. "If a thing didn't work this way, we'd try it that way."

On the night of the fight, I stopped by the out-of-town newsstand in Times Square on my way to Madison Square Garden and bought a copy of the Providence *Evening Bulletin*. It carried a first-page story on the fight by Mike Thomas, the *Bulletin*'s boxing writer, who not unnaturally picked Araujo to win, "home-town view or not." Mike had written, "He should take the decision over the titleholder, Jimmy Carter of the Bronx, in their 15-round go at Madison Square Garden. But there is the distinct possibility he could win on a knockout by the 12th or 13th round. That is, if his plan of speed first and then explosion is not disturbed. He figures to start bombing by the 10th or 11th. By then, the champion ought to be set up for the kill." Thomas said that more than three thousand Rhode Islanders were coming down for the fight. I am not a Rhode Islander, but I had a lot of fun working there, and I had become as partisan as any of them.

I had plenty of time, so I walked on past the Garden to the Capitol Hotel, which I figured would be Providence headquarters because Araujo was staying there. The curb in front of the place was parked solid with cars bearing Rhode Island license plates, and the sidewalk between the cars and the hotel was covered with feet more accustomed to the pavements of Dorrance and Westminster Streets. The air was musical with the flattened "a"s and squeezed "e"s of southern New England speech; a man smoking a pipe to maintain his cam told me that patties had come on by caa and bus as well as by special train. "We've taken over the town," he said modestly, removing his pipe from his mouth and waving it bravely in the direction of the eight million beyond the stockade of automobiles. I stood around for a while, half expecting to see somebody I knew, and then left to rejoin my fellow aborigines.

When I walked into the Garden, a Berber from Morocco was in the ring, whacking away ineffectually at a long, stringy Negro from Cuba; it seemed unbelievable that two men could have come so far to fight so little. The Berber and the Negro banged away awkwardly for a couple more rounds and then disappeared, after one of the least important decisions of the century. Next, a short but barrel-chested Puerto Rican lightweight came on with a thin fellow from Philadelphia; the weights were even, and it was a contest between a vertical line and a cube. This was better—the Philadelphian was resolute, although unduly prolonged, and the Puerto Rican appeared to be a great hitter, in a shot-putting style. "Look at him!" a man behind me cried. "He looks like a monkey—you know, a griller." Having found his *mot juste*, he stuck to it for eight rounds. "A griller!" he would exclaim whenever the Puerto Rican would up to pitch a fist. "A griller! A griller!" The griller did not succeed in converting the Philadelphian into a horizontal, but he made him look like two sides of a triangle in search of a third. "A griller!" the man in back of me said in awe when the boxers left the ring.

The hands of the Garden clock were now so near ten, the mystic hour of television, that the Garden's baritone soloist had to sing the national anthem at the tempo of "The Darktown Strutters' Ball." The heroes of the evening entered the ring without the draggy solemnity that used to enhance the dignity of the beginning of a championship fight. The sponsor was paying fifty thousand dollars for radio and television rights, considerably more than the match was expected to attract at the gate. (It drew thirty-eight thousand dollars.) Carter was longer, leaner, blacker, and older than Araujo—he was twenty-nine— and wore a white robe on the back of which was lettered, with unexpected formality, "James Carter." He had a kind of desiccated look that I mistook for evidence of brittleness. When Johnny Addie, the announcer, introduced Araujo, there was a thunderous cheer from the Rhode Islanders. They greeted Carter with equally thunderous boos. The visitors must have made up half the audience.

At the bell Araujo came out on his toes and started circling Carter, jabbing his left to the champion's face as the taller man advanced. They were flicking, fast jabs, usually double, like a cat striking twice at a butterfly, and, since George was generally going away when they landed, they were not stiff enough to set Carter back on his heels. If I had not read the *Bulletin*, I would have thought our man had an exaggerated respect for Carter's hitting power, but I knew the battle plan. As the round went on, I thought George looked a good bet. He was on his toes all the way, bouncing wastefully, but his legs were marvels; that kind of underpinning is an asset to be exploited, like reach or hitting power. And he was not using his legs to carry him in one direction; he was moving in and out of range and hitting repeatedly. Carter, bent slightly forward, with his elbows high, moved steadily after him, feet flat on the mat, a perfect picture of the deadly hitter I had been assured he wasn't. He had, in fact, knocked out only a small percentage of his opponents up to the previous April twenty-fourth, when he boxed an unfortunate youth named Tommy Collins, in Boston, and bowled him over ten times before the referee stopped the fight. That may have convinced him he could hit. In the first round, though, Carter was missing and George was hitting, and I have never been the kind of fight-goer who gives a fighter credit for chasing an opponent and getting hit.

I was relieved to find that the man and woman in front of me were of my persuasion in this matter, for there is nothing less agreeable to me than having to turn my attention from the ring to explain the rudimentary principles of the sweet science to my fellow customers. At the end of the round I penciled a large "1" on a sheet of yellow paper I had on my knee and marked next to it a large "A." The woman, who had been peeping over her shoulder, smiled and said, "I agree with you exactly." At the end of the next round I marked "2—E," for "even," and the lady said, "Right." In the third Carter caught George in a neutral corner and landed a few solid raps. With an impartiality that aroused my own admiration, I marked "3—C." But in the fourth and fifth, things went so well for Providence that it looked to me "as safe as the Bank," to borrow a phrase from Pierce Egan, the Thucydides of the London prize ring. The mahogany boy opened a cut over Carter's right eye, and in the fifth he began hitting him with left hooks to the stomach. Carter ended the body attack by crouching lower and bringing down his elbows, but he was no nearer nailing Araujo than he had been at the beginning of the fight. They had now covered a third of the course, and it wasn't until the tenth or eleventh round that Araujo was even supposed to open up with his heavy guns. For the moment, I thought Carter might not get that far. But Carter's seconds stopped the blood from the cut and he got going again, while Araujo, gradually coming down from his toes, seemed to take a breather. After both the sixth and seventh rounds I marked a "C," and it occurred to me that just as a man might convince himself he was a hitter by acting like a hitter, so might his opponent fall victim to the same delusion by taking the man at his own valuation. Here were two men of equal weight, equally hard to hurt and, in their records, almost equally damaging punchers—Araujo had actually scored more knockouts in fifty-two bouts than Carter had in eighty-two. Yet the fight was falling into the pattern of a match between a boxer and a puncher, or a light man and a heavy man.

In the eighth the Providence hope did better, beating Carter to the punch, cutting his eye again, and making him look slow, old, and angry. As the hand of the big clock timing the rounds swept past a minute and a half it appeared to me that we were ahead at the halfway mark of the fight, although not far enough to mean anything. The ninth started like every round before it, with Araujo moving and stabbing, landing a succession of those double flicks to the face. Carter hit him with a right to the body that landed below the line. The referee warned the dark, persistent fellow, and then Carter lashed out with a right to the jaw, over that left hand Araujo insisted on carrying low. The boy may have dropped it still lower in involuntary reaction to the body punch. There were a couple more punches, and then Araujo was on the mat. He bounced up almost as soon as he hit the floor. Now, when he was hurt, instead of moving out of danger as he had been doing all evening, he leaped at Carter like a kid in a schoolyard. He went down again, came up again, slugged some more, and then, just before the end of the round, took a wicked right-hander to the jaw that had him wandering aimlessly at the bell.

An older, or a less well-conditioned, boxer would not have lasted out the first thirty seconds of the tenth, but Araujo, moving uncertainly at first, got back on his toes and boxed. He lost the round, of course, but he opened Carter's cut again. The eleventh was even more trying for him, but in the twelfth he seemed completely recovered, jabbing, dancing, and generally fooling the older man, who was beginning to look tired. At the end of the round, I marked my first "A" since the

eighth, but the boy was now so far behind on points that he
would have to do something sensational to win the decision in
three more rounds.

Travis's *Wunderkind* went out to do it in the thirteenth, and
for a couple of minutes, changing his style completely, he slugged
with Carter, usually beating him in exchanges. The crowd, which
always prefers slugging to boxing, roared approval, and this
time not only the Rhode Islanders were cheering. But, like
Larry's kick the day he was stretched, George's gesture was all
pride. Carter caught him with another series of punches, he
went down again, and the referee stopped the fight, after two
minutes and sixteen seconds of the thirteenth round.

The last thing I remember about the fight is Travis's face as
he hauled himself through the ropes to get his boy. It is a big
face, and it was wide open, as if he had just seen something he
couldn't believe. I don't know what kind of journey home the
fellows from Providence had, but I imagine it was quiet.

On the following Sunday morning, I called Travis at his
hotel to find out why things had turned out so, and he said to
come right over; he would be waiting for me in the lobby.
"George is with me," he said. When I got there, the Capitol,
which had been buzzing with Rhode Islanders on fight night,
was as quiet as a training camp in the Adirondacks. It is a big
place, built to be a hotel for the Knights of Columbus, who
lost it to the infidels during the Depression, but for some reason the fellow who designed it gave it a lobby no larger than
the front room of a police station. Araujo, looking rather sub-
dued, was wearing a sports jacket and slacks. His face was
somewhat swollen, and he was even less talkative than he had
been before the fight. Travis, like a father who knows his boy
has made mistakes but is willing to forgive him, said Araujo
had been following instructions by boxing with Carter in the
early rounds. "If you're a fighter, and I'm a fighter and boxer,
why should I go along with you at your game from the start?"
he asked. "Isn't it better if I box you the first nine or ten
rounds and cut you? Then I can come on to win. That's what
we were planning to do," he added, confirming the battle plan
in the *Evening Bulletin*. "It was working, too. George had him
cut pretty good. But just when I was going to open George

up, we hit the bad luck. He got knocked down, and, never being used to it, he jumped right up. That was stupid!" he said to Araujo. "It was a stupid thing to do."

"I was just angry and excited," the boy said. "I lost my head."

"The bad luck was that he went down with his back toward his corner," said Travis. "If he could have seen us, we would have motioned to him to stay down. If he had taken nine, his head would have been clear, and meanwhile Carter would have had to walk to a neutral corner. George would have gone on the bicycle as soon as he got up, and we would have been all right again before the end of the round."

"Couldn't you have yelled to him?" I asked.

"He couldn't have heard us," the manager said. "In Providence, I might take a chance and run around the ring to where he could see me, but here they might disqualify us for that. And when he got knocked down the second time, he had his back to us again."

"It was my own fault," Araujo said. "I was going good, my wind was fine. In another round, I was going to start to take him."

"It's one of the things we can't ever prove, George," said Travis. "When you bounced up, it was the turning point. I was amazed."

Sammy Richman, Araujo's New York manager, who wandered in just then, had a less tactical, more general explanation. "He didn't make his fight because he was too excited," he said. "You know—too pent up."

NINO AND A NANIMAL

IN the spring of 1954 Whitey Bimstein and Freddie Brown told me about a new talent confided to their care who was *outré* but interesting. "A nanimal," Mr. Bimstein said. "A throwback to the man of the gutter." "A mental case," Mr. Brown agreed, without disapproval in his voice. "By that I mean he's got to be doing something all the time." Managers, like book publishers, make most of the money, but trainers, like editors, participate more directly in the artists' labors. Bimstein and Brown are editors of prizefighters. Mediocrity depresses them; they are excited by talent, even latent. What they dream about is genius, but unfortunately that is harder to identify.

Technically, Whitey and Freddie can do a lot for a fighter— excise redundant gesture and impose a severe logic of punching, as demonstrable as old-fashioned mathematics. When I walked into Stillman's gymnasium one day, for example, Freddie was tutoring a pale, big-boned boy at least as strong as a policeman's horse. ("Strength, most undoubtedly, is what a boxer ought to start out with," wrote Pierce Egan, the Holinshed of the London prize ring, "but without art he will succeed but poorly.") "Throw a left hook," Freddie would say. The boy would pull his left elbow back to a line even with his hip, and Freddie would slap him on the left side of the face and push. "What happened?" Freddie would ask. "I don't know," the boy would say. And Freddie would say, "All right, throw a left hook." The boy would pull his left elbow back again and they would go through the same performance. When Freddie finally saw that the Socratic method was no go, he said wearily, "You dropped your shoulder and I come over it is what happened. Hook with your elbow in." He demonstrated what he meant. After he had sent the boy upstairs to do body exercises, he said to me, "He had a couple of fights in Canada, can you imagine? Up there it is like the amateurs." The next time I visited the gym, the boy wasn't there. He was back in Canada, I imagine.

It is the psyche that makes Freddie and Whitey sweat. Like authors, fighters of exemplary moral quality may be bores. And fighters who do a lot of beautiful things nobody else does may be children emotionally. The good boys get married. The bad ones get in jams. It is hard to tell which may mean more trouble for a trainer. "The worst trouble is assorted maniacs," Whitey says, "because you never know when it is going to break out." A fellow Whitey and Freddie know named Maurie Waxman had a fighter who could move almost as well as Benny Leonard, but he habitually lost his prey. As soon as the other fellow showed signs of damage, Waxman's fighter would back away. One night, in the ring with a tough Puerto Rican, Waxman's fighter hit his opponent in the first round, at which, according to Whitey, "the guy's eye come up like a grape." After that, Waxman's fighter refrained so studiously from hitting the eye that the other fellow made up much of the ground he had lost. Just before the last round, Waxman leaned over his fighter and said, "Julie, I ain't cruel, but just a *touch* on that eye would do it." The fighter looked up at his manager and said, "Maurie, I'm sorry, but I can't. I'm allergic to blood." In relating this to me, Whitey said, "That must of been a nice time to find *that* out." But where you suspect genius, you've got to go along. A harsh insistence on conventional methods may spoil an original style.

I have known Whitey for more than twenty years (he had been a trainer for fifteen years before that), and by now I can tell from looking at him whether he thinks genius is lurking just the other side of the horizon. Four years ago he was desperate for talent. Prosperity had ruined the future, he said; any kid just out of school could get a job for sixty dollars a week, and as a consequence dilettantism was rife in boxing. The faintest frown of fortune would send a boy back to well-paid labor. Boys boxed only to attain social prestige. "Garbage," Whitey said then, when I asked him about the season's vintage. But this spring he was wearing the expression of an editor who has found two new poets and a woman novelist with an acid talent. The mild recession was not solely responsible, he said, although it had made the boys more serious about boxing as a vocation. He and Freddie had three good fighters training at once—two lightweights and one around '30 (130 pounds) who could do '26 to qualify as a featherweight. They also had this animal, Whitey said, who ran fifteen or twenty miles a day on the road and would box fifteen rounds every day if they would let him. Whitey was in the position of the late Max Perkins, with a handful of good established writers and a Thomas Wolfe in training in Brooklyn.

I asked him how big the animal was, and he said it was a colored heavyweight, six feet one and a half and over '90. "His name is Tommy Jackson," he said. "Until you know him, you don't know what you got to put up with." Freddie joined us and said it was a shame they had television. "This kid is still two or three years away," he said, "but how can a learner eat when television's killed off most of the small clubs? The only money is the feature, so they got to fight features or quit. This fellow had fifteen fights and then they made him with Rex Layne and Clarence Henry. Dog eat dog." I asked how the animal had made out against Layne and Henry, and Whitey said he had won big, but the trouble was now he had to keep on meeting name fighters. "How does he fight?" I asked. "He throws a lot of leather," Whitey said. "Like a noctopus!" Whitey is a small man—he used to be what he calls a bantyweight—with a rosy face and white eyelashes. His face and features are small in proportion to his head, and this gives him the look of a medium-old baby, which is disconcerting when he hasn't shaved for a couple of days. "He takes the best punch in the business," Freddie said. "The best thing he has is endurance." Freddie, an ex-featherweight, is bigger than Whitey and has a broken nose. I gathered from the two of them that Jackson won his fights by inducing exhaustion in his opponents, who collapsed like men worn out from slapping at horseflies. He stopped them without knocking them down.

As he talked about Jackson, Whitey looked a trifle self-conscious. "He is a ninstinctive fighter," he said. "He imitates what the other fellow does." "Can't you teach him anything?" I asked, and Freddie said, "Yeah, we are teaching him not to jab with his palms up, which he did so in case he changed his mind he would be ready to uppercut." Shortly after that I read in the paper that Jackson had stopped a fellow named Bucceroni; it was another case of exhaustion.

The first time I saw Jackson, it was on television and he was fighting a small heavyweight named Jimmy Slade, a trickster. Jackson did what I had been told to expect, but Slade didn't collapse. He cuffed Jackson around and made him look silly. I thought this might be good for Jackson, as his managers might now drop him back into his own sort of competition, where he would have a chance to practice. Instead, they got him a match in Madison Square Garden with a fellow named Norkus, whom he stopped, although he didn't knock him down. Managers have to eat, too. But they didn't take Slade again. Meanwhile the sports writers had adopted Jackson—whom they called Hurricane—as a dull-day subject. They said he couldn't read or write, made up songs, had a punch called the double uppercut, and blamed the Slade defeat on too much fresh air

inhaled during roadwork. What attracted them most, I suspect, was the recurrent sports-page myth of the man who can
do a complicated thing without learning how. It is an old
dream of childhood, and, while it never comes true, people
like to read about it.

At Stillman's, after the Norkus fight, I was puzzled to find
that Whitey and Freddie themselves were taking Jackson seriously. At least they said they were. The Slade defeat, Freddie
said, had been due to an intense but ephemeral romance, followed by a debauch. "Jackson drunk five bottles of Coca-Cola
before going into the ring," he said. "Naturally, that slowed
him up starting. But in the last round he was getting to Slade."
"A nanimal," Whitey said. "You don't know what you got to
put up with." But now Whitey and Freddie had persuaded him
to swear off soft drinks until after fights, they said, and his
mother had broken up the romance. "Mentally, he was below
par for Slade," Freddie said, opening new vistas of horror.
"He's better now." We stood beside Stillman's No. 1 ring and
watched Jackson work, and also the three good boys—Arthur
Persley, a colored lightweight, who had an engagement with an
Algerian fighter in Atlantic City; Davey Gallardo, a California-
Mexican feather, who had a bout coming up in Philadelphia;
and Cisco Andrada, another Mexican-American, from Comp-
ton, a suburb of Los Angeles. Andrada, like Persley, is a lightweight. He was going to make his New York debut at St.
Nick's, Whitey said, and he earnestly advised me to be present.
"You will want to say you was there," he said. "He's got everything." All three young men, I noticed, boxed in accordance
with the classical verities. They punctuated jabs with hooks,
and hooks with crosses, and they uppercut with one hand at a
time.

After the workout we all went back to the honeycomb of
beaverboard partitions that constitutes the private deluxe
dressing rooms at Stillman's. Each one is ornamented by a
large sign, reading, "WASH YOUR CLOTHES—BY ORDER OF
THE ATHLETIC COMMISSION." It was a hot day, and Whitey
stripped to his shorts and rubbed his charges, one by one—a
chore that he usually delegates to his assistant, a fat man named
Coco. When Whitey takes over, it means he thinks he has something special. Gallardo had been working against extra-tall

sparring partners, because the boy he was going to fight in Philadelphia was tall, and also, from the long view, because Sandy Saddler, the world's featherweight champion, is abnormally tall for his weight. Andrada had been working with strong boys, since his opponent at St. Nick's was a crowding type who was expected to have a few pounds on him. Persley, Gallardo, and Andrada are boys who have been to high school, and, as Whitey says, "they talk nice." No maniacs. Whitey kneaded them with esteem.

When Whitey got Jackson on the table, though, the animal began to squeal and laugh. "I'm so ticklish," he said. "Maybe that's why I fight so good." He has a small head, a long, cylindrical torso of no great diameter for a heavyweight, legs like a high jumper's, and long, powerful arms. His skin is a dark-plum color. "I was born under a pine tree," he said. "Maybe that's why I fight so good." I had heard he was raised at Rockaway Beach, where most boys skip school to go swimming, so I asked him if he liked to swim in the surf. "Not me," he said. "I got drowned in an undertow." Subsequent answers were no more illuminating. He looked disturbed, and then the reason for his preoccupation appeared. "Freddie," he said, "get me my wallet. Those nosy rats always lookin' in it." Brown brought him the wallet, and he sat up and spread some money on his knee. "The money is all there, Hurricane," Freddie said. "Twenty-four dollars." Hurricane shuffled the bills cunningly and said, "That's correct. Twenty-four." Whitey slapped him on the back and told him to turn over, and Jackson turned over, putting the wallet under his belly. After Jackson had dressed and gone I asked the partners what they thought he would do to Rocky Marciano if the two should meet. "He could cut him to pieces," Whitey said, and Freddie nodded. Now I know why a lot of the books that get published do. Optimism is the besetting disease of all lovers of the arts.

The I.B.C., however, had already made Jackson with Nino Valdes, a Cuban heavyweight whose personality is more arresting than his workmanship, which is heavy and conventional, like a Spanish dessert. Valdes is very big—he generally fights at about two hundred and eight pounds—and highly experienced, but he has a reputation for laziness. Encountering Charlie

Goldman, who edits Marciano, I asked him for an *expertise* on the forthcoming Jackson-Valdes fight, and he said that the Cuban's geniality had led people to underrate him. "He does a few good things, but after he does them, he loafs in between," Charlie said. "Jackson won't let him loaf, so Valdes will kill him."

The next time I saw Jackson was in the offices of the New York State Athletic Commission, at 226 West 47th Street, a few days before the fight. Many of the fights in the Garden in summer are virtually studio shows for television, but the I.B.C. hoped to get some flesh-and-blood customers for this one. Valdes and Jackson had been sent to out-of-town training camps to underline the significance of the match; if Hurricane butchered the Cuban, he would be considered worthy of a fight with Marciano for the world's championship, a press release said. Now the pair had been brought into town for a physical examination, although both fighters were as healthy as mandrills.

When I entered the waiting room outside the office of the Commission's medical examiner I saw Sammy Golden, one of the three men who split Jackson's contract—thirty-three and a third per cent each way. Golden is a diminished, skinny old manager who hasn't had any luck since a fighter named Georgie Ward retired in 1923. Ward was a real good welterweight and is now a cop in New Jersey. I like to talk to Golden, because I know a fellow who used to fight Ward on odd Saturdays in Boston. (On even Thursdays they would fight in Newark.) This time we had barely exchanged greetings when a man named Lippy Breidbart came up behind me and plucked at my sleeve. Breidbart also owned a third of the animal. He is a fattish man who dresses sharp.

I asked Golden whether it was true that Jackson could neither read nor write.

"Ask me," Breidbart said. "I'm the manager. Every time I look at a paper, Sammy is making a quotation. He is strictly Georgie Ward, he lives in the past. The answer is Jackson can read and write, but not good."

"*You're* the manager?" Golden said with spirit. "We should never have took you in."

"Shut your mouth!" Breidbart said. "You're an old man." His tone implied that only Golden's decrepitude protected him.

At this point, Frank Leonetti, the third owner, came up and turned on Breidbart. Golden withdrew to a far corner of the room and made faces. Leonetti is a bulky, bull-necked man, a division superintendent on a bus line, and it was he who discovered Jackson down at Rockaway Beach. "When you make a move, you don't tell us," he said. "You think that's nice?"

"That's a perposterous statement!" Breidbart said.

"Any time I made a perposterous statement, you let me know about it!" Leonetti shouted, shoving Breidbart with his belly.

Breidbart was the manager of record, which means he was the one authorized by the Athletic Commission to make matches and sign contracts for the fighter. He was now advancing the contention that he also had the sole right to make statements. Jackson, who had joined us, put his hands on the shoulders of the two quarreling men. "Why can't you guys get along?" he asked. "I'm the fighter. I'm the one should do the worrying, not you." He turned to Freddie Brown, who had brought him into town on a bus from his training quarters at Greenwood Lake, New York. "I don't like it here," Jackson said. "I want to go back to the mountains, shoot a mouse. No mouses here."

"You can't go back now," Brown said in a soothing voice. Then he turned to me. "Hurricane found a new interest," he said. "He shoots rats with a twenty-two. He calls them mice."

"Mouses," the fighter corrected him. "I shoot them between the eyes." He seemed depressed.

"He finds them on the dump," Freddie said.

When Jackson saw that Freddie wasn't going to take him back to the mountains, he wandered away and sat down, morosely staring at his feet.

"I don't know where he gets the energy," said Freddie, who looked underweight. "The hardest worker I ever seen before him is Marciano, but Marciano works steady and then he rests good. Also he eats good. Jackson don't sleep enough and he don't eat enough. These boys that ain't used to good food, it don't agree with them."

"What kind of food is he used to?" I asked.

"He wants hot dogs," Freddie said. "And also ice cream and pie. We got him to accept hamburgers as a substitute, but you got to watch him all the time. He fell out of a canoe which I had told him not to get into it, and he can't swim good. He wants to ride a horse, he thinks he is Eddie Arcaro. And he could easy shoot himself instead of them rats." Freddie shuddered.

Valdes and his manager, Bobby Gleason, had observed the ruckus between the three owners with polite amusement, like members of Miss Hewitt's Classes visiting a school for delinquent children. "The board of stragedy is having a tough time," Gleason said when I walked over to them. Gleason is a stocky man who runs a gymnasium for prizefighters in the Bronx. Valdes is the color of blond mahogany, and his shoulders look as wide as a door. He was wearing a raspberry steamer cap, a pink silk shirt (18 neck, 37 sleeves), and white pants. Gold teeth provided extra flash. Valdes and Gleason communicate in a lingua franca of English, Neapolitan, and Spanish, and Gleason interprets for others when he thinks it advisable. "Mucho wise guy, Bobby," Valdes says.

When Valdes took the pink shirt off in the medical examiner's office, we could see that he was wearing a gold chain with an amulet around his eighteen-inch neck, which he considers his most impressive feature. He got the neck by carrying three-hundred-and-thirty-pound sacks of sugar on his head when he was a boy. It makes him look slightly pinheaded. Dr. Vincent Nardiello, the examining physician, had the fighters spread their arms, so that he could measure their reach, and it made a good shot for the photographers, who ordered them to go through numerous repeats. Valdes said something in Spanish to Gleason. "He wants to know which one they are measuring for a casket," Gleason told me. The Cuban was six feet three, an inch and a half taller than Jackson, but Jackson had longer arms. Jackson, who had continued to look glum, cheered up for a minute when Dr. Nardiello allowed him to listen to his own heart through the stethoscope. "It sounds good!" he shouted. "Solid!" But soon he was pouting again. In the elevator, going down to the street, he closed his eyes and allowed his chin to droop on his chest, while he leaned his

weight on Freddie Brown. "I don't like three men over me,"
he said. "If you don't take me back to the mountains, I'm
going back alone."

Two days later, I heard that Jackson had run away from the
mountains, because Freddie wouldn't let him ride a horse, and
had reported to Whitey at Stillman's. Whitey had stayed there
to handle the three bright boys. Jackson was like a child of di-
vorce running from one parent to the other. When Jackson
got to Stillman's, Whitey told me afterward, he said, "This is
where I feel at home. No country air in my belly."

On the night of the fight, I was more excited than I had
been before any match for years, and for purely subjective reasons. If the animal won, it meant that the Sweet Science was
mere guesswork, requiring not even a specialized intelligence.
It would be quite a different thing from the victories of im-
mortals like Griffo and Dutch Sam, who were irresponsibles
only when they were *outside* the ring. There have been plenty
of musicians and painters who didn't have much sense otherwise, and Dostoevski was a political imbecile. I had nothing
against Jackson *qua* Jackson, and I wished Whitey and Freddie
all kinds of luck with their more conventional clients, but if the
animal could beat even a fair fighter, it meant that two hundred and fifty years of painfully acquired experience had been
lost to the human race; science was a washout and art a vanity,
and Freddie and Whitey had queered their own game.

The preliminaries were unusually good and, from my point
of view, reassuring. A tough-looking middleweight from York-
ville, named Schulz, knocked out a boy from Chicago with a
short, economical right to the jaw—one out of the book. A
dark, knowledgeable featherweight from Harlem prevailed
tactically and strategically over a Fighting Newsboy from
Columbus, Ohio, who punched in wider arcs. The Fighting
Newsboy did not attempt to upset the artistic canon; he simply
operated too near its edge. The ancient laws appeared still to
be operative when the principals entered the ring for the feature bout. We sang the national anthem, as usual.

Whitey, Freddie, and Breidbart all came into the ring with
their primitive. Jackson weighed a hundred and ninety and a

half, which indicated that he had overdone his self-induced training sessions. Valdes's weight was announced as two hundred and four, which showed that he had done more work than customary, but not too much. In the first round Valdes, boxing straight up, moved forward methodically and punched at Jackson's body. Jackson, fidgeting about, did not accomplish anything. A Cuban sitting next to me, possibly a political exile, said happily, "Well, Valdes gets cut up tonight, no?" Valdes is for Batista. There was no sign that it would happen.

Jackson stood up in his corner halfway through the one-minute rest period and did what gym teachers call "running in place," at the same time waving his arms. When the bell rang, he rushed out to meet Valdes, dabbing and slapping. Valdes took aim like a bowler and knocked him through the ropes, at which point, since Jackson's body was very nearly horizontal, the referee should have started a count, in my opinion, even though the lower strand prevented the animal's body from touching the canvas. Valdes—"mucho nice boy," as he would have said—turned and went to a neutral corner. The referee disentangled Jackson and upended him, and Valdes knocked him down again a couple of times. Each time Jackson fell—he did even that grotesquely, landing once sitting, once kneeling—he bounced up at the count of two or three. But the referee, because of a fairly new rule of the New York State Athletic Commission, had to stand in front of him and count eight before permitting the opponents to resume action. According to a collateral rule, if one boxer knocks the other down three times in one round, the referee has to stop the fight. (This is well intentioned but silly, because a boxer like Jackson, who doesn't know what to do with his feet, can be knocked down several times without being hurt much, while a fellow who is helpless but remains upright takes a beating without respite, the kind that is most likely to end in permanent injury. It has long been within the referee's discretion to stop a fight at any time, and that's the way the matter should have been left.) By my reckoning—and I was not alone—the second knockdown was really the third, and the referee, Al Berl, should consequently have stopped the fight there if he was going to be a precisionist. But Berl let them go to it again. Jackson was fluttering like a winged bird, making a difficult though harmless target, and Valdes, conscious of the three-knockdown rule, was following him about, eager to bring him down, even for a half second, before the round ended. Valdes has had many fights, has always finished strong, and was in good condition, but he seemed at this point to be heaving. Perhaps it was merely emotion, for he could not have anticipated a chance to knock off work so early. Several times he aimed as deliberately as if he were about to hurl a sack of sugar at a toad but missed. Finally he missed Jackson's head with his right fist and, in recovering, hit him on the back of the neck with his forearm, as big around as a normal collar. He may simply have been trying to keep himself from falling. Anyway, Jackson's knees hit the floor, and Berl, perhaps to compensate for the time he hadn't counted, flung his arms wide in token of a technical knockout. Jackson promptly jumped up. In Pierce Egan's time the victor might have offered to knock the loser out again to satisfy him, but that was before the Athletic Commission. (I know an old boxer who was awarded a fight on a foul because the other fellow was biting him. My friend was enjoying himself, so he said he would go on with the match if the fellow would promise to stop biting. The opponent promised, but he didn't keep his word. "Maybe he hadn't ate lately," my man says.) Gleason towed Valdes into the corner of the ring farthest from Jackson and, snuggling against his flank, made him hold up his right hand for the benefit of the photographers, who got a picture like one of those circus shots taken under the elephant's trunk. From the way Valdes was grinning, he had a pretty good program lined up for the rest of the evening.

Meanwhile Jackson was standing in his corner, shaking his head and refusing to leave the ring. He demanded the privilege of being hit some more. I could see Whitey and Freddie and a policeman arguing with him, and then they were joined by Dr. Nardiello, for whom I imagine Jackson has a lot of respect since the incident of the stethoscope. At last they persuaded him to leave.

After an early ending like that most of the customers stay to watch the four-round "emergency" bout that is put on as a postscript. I watched a couple of rounds of it myself. One of the principals had been an early professional opponent of Jackson's a scant twenty months back. On the basis of what I saw, I can't figure how Jackson beat him.

The show had drawn forty-five hundred cash customers—possibly six thousand in all, including deadheads, but even that is only a third of the Garden's capacity, and there was no trouble getting around. The evening seemed so incomplete that I decided to visit Jackson's dressing room, off the corridor on the north side of the arena, to hear the losing faction's story. There were perhaps twenty colored people outside the door, including several attractive girls. As I approached, the door flew open, and Jackson, dressed and carrying a suitcase, dashed through the group and ran up the stairs that lead to an exit on 50th Street, about midway between Eighth and Ninth Avenues. "Tommy, come back!" one of the girls yelled. I followed Jackson out, not knowing quite what he might do, and ran slap into a storm, of which I had been unaware. It was a short, intense squall that had just hit the city, and it seemed to me an exaggerated reaction to the defeat of Tommy Jackson. To him, however, marching off into the rain, it may have seemed a fitting recognition of the occasion. He turned south on Ninth, and my curiosity was not strong enough to draw me more than a short distance into the rain after him. Then I began working my way back toward Eighth, taking advantage of intervening marquees and saloons for cover. At Muller's, on the north side of the street, they have Münchner beer on tap, and I sheltered there longer than at any other place. By the time I got around to the main entrance of the Garden the storm had died to a drizzle, but there were still a couple of dozen fight people under the big marquee talking about the night's events. I saw a second named Izzy Blanc, who had worked a pair of the minor bouts, and asked him if he knew what had happened to Jackson. "He's walking around the Garden in the rain," he said. "He's been around ten times since I've been standing here." We waited, and within a minute Jackson swung by—silent, head forward, looking like a priest who has found he has no vocation or like an actor hissed from the stage.

I asked Izzy if he had seen the disputed knockdown, but he, a diplomat, offered a good alibi. "After the second knockdown I was on my way to the dressing room," he said. "I had the emergency." He meant he had been engaged to second one of the boxers in the final four-rounder, and he had sensed that it was going to be needed earlier than anybody had expected. "I had my back to the ring," he said.

The rain was easy to ignore now, and Izzy said he was going to walk up Eighth, stopping by a couple of bars where he might meet other fight people. "We'll probably find Whitey at the Neutral Corner," he said. The Neutral is a bar on the southwest corner of 55th and Eighth, and when we got there, Whitey was on a stool smoking a cigar and having a glass of beer. "If they want to rune boxing," he said, "that's the way to do it. He wrastled him to the ground just when the kid was hitting his stride."

"His what?" I said.

"Sure," Bimstein said. "He was just beginning to come on good."

"How about the first three knockdowns?" I asked.

"There was only one knockdown," Whitey said. He rejected my proposition that Berl had let the animal off the time he got knocked through the ropes. "And the second thing he called a knockdown, that was a push, too," Whitey said. He appeared calm, not bitter, and acted as if it were a matter of little moment to him if the Commission wanted to take the bread out of its own mouth. "He was just sizing the fellow up," he said. "And the fellow trips him, and boom, Berl stops the fight." I began to suspect we hadn't seen the same fight that evening.

SOIRÉE INTIME

WHILE reading the newspaper Froissarts' stories the day after the first Marciano-Charles fight in the summer of 1954, I noticed that there was to be another bout that evening, at Madison Square Garden. This one had been kept so deep a secret during the days leading up to the big match that my discovery made me feel I was getting in on something like a stag show. Even in Tex Rickard's palmy days as a promoter at the Garden, he would never have ventured a show on the night following one of his own ball-park promotions. The theory was that the average fight fan, having spent his money for a big ticket, would have nothing left for a little ticket the same week. This card, however, had a television sponsor, the Gillette Razor Blade Company, and so was economically independent. (The I.B.C. had kept the Marciano-Charles bout off television in the metropolitan district, which had undoubtedly helped the gate.)

The Garden card looked fairly promising, on paper. In the main bout, Orlando Zulueta, the lightweight champion of Cuba, was to meet a fellow named Johnny Gonsalves, out of Oakland, California, who, according to the brief press notices, ranked as one of the best lightweights in the United States. (After what I saw, I hoped he wasn't.) I had never seen Gonsalves, but in 1948 I had seen Zulueta fight in Havana, in the Cuban equivalent of the Garden. That had been for the featherweight championship of Cuba, which has sent out some excellent fighting men in the lighter classes, and his opponent had been an established Havana star named Acevedo, a light-skinned Cuban with a sandy mustache, exceedingly *caballero*. I remembered Zulueta—a tall, thin, dark young Negro with a beautifully educated left hand. He had been on his way up, and Acevedo at the top of the downgrade. The hall was packed with a noisy crowd, jeering and imploring. It was carnival time, very gay. Zulueta had made a fool of Acevedo for a couple of rounds. Then, affected by the carnival spirit, he had stopped stabbing and started slugging with the older man. This had gone well at first, but the Acevedo had nailed him with a few good punches. Most of the crowd was with the old champion, and Zulueta's seconds were yelling frantically. Without understanding technical Spanish, I had known what they were saying: "Stay away from him and box!" He had gone back to boxing, survived the round, and given his man a good pasting. At the end, the judges awarded the decision to Acevedo—as rank a miscarriage of justice as I have seen outside of the Dominican Republic. I remembered that Acevedo's manager carried him around the ring, pickaback, seven times.

Since there was no large sum involved as admission fee, I decided to attend the Garden bout as a customer, a *cochon de payant*. The first preliminary was, as usual, scheduled to go on at eight-thirty. I arrived at the Eighth Avenue entrance to the Garden at a quarter to nine and found the place deserted, except for three men at the orange-drink stand in the lobby and four more talking baseball under the marquee. The marquee at least confirmed the report that a fight was supposed to take place that evening. Scouting around among the ticket windows, I found one that was open. The man behind it was reading the next day's entries at Aqueduct, but he looked up when I said "Pardon me." I asked if he had a good ringside seat left, and he looked at me a bit oddly and said, "Second row, right in the center." I asked him how much, and he said "Eight dollars," in a tone that implied he expected me to go away. He may have thought I had mistaken the place for a movie house.

As I entered the door to the Garden proper, I thought I saw the statue of Joe Gans, the old lightweight champion, smile gratefully. The ticket taker, one of the gruff old retired cops who usually look at me as if I were personally responsible for their hurting feet, said, "Nice weather we're having, ain't it?" The program sellers, who ordinarily snarl at you if you can't find the right change, looked so happy to see me that I handed one of them a twenty-dollar bill, just to test his reaction. He counted out the change like a little gentleman, saying, "Nineteen-seventy-five. Right? I'm sorry I have to give you so many singles, Mister." At the beer bar, on other occasions so crowded, I could have been served instantly. Unfortunately, I wasn't thirsty. In the inner lobby, I saw nobody I recognized from the fight mob; no self-respecting character would accept a free ticket that was easy to get. Murray Goodman, the press agent for the I.B.C., entered from the arena, recognized me, and looked as if I had caught him in a humiliating situation. "I gotta be here," he said. "It's my job."

"Is it going to be a hell of a fight?" I asked.

He looked at me suspiciously. "They must think it'll sell razor blades," he said.

A sallow bystander said hello, and Mr. Goodman introduced him to me as Hymie Wallman, Zulueta's manager. Mr. Wallman had been watching the door, and I hoped for his sake that he had not been trying to calculate the gate, because nobody had come in since me. "What percentage are you working on?" I asked, to cheer him up.

"What difference what percentage?" Mr. Wallman inquired bitterly. "You kidding?"

"Hymie isn't doing so bad," Mr. Goodman said cheerily. "He gets four thousand for his fighter from television. The other fighter gets four thousand, too. The gate receipts are like a tip."

"Yeah? Wonderful," said Mr. Wallman. "You were up at that fight last night?" he asked me. I said I had been, and he said, "If this fight tonight wasn't on television, it would draw fifty thousand dollars." Wiping a tear from the corner of my eye, I said good-by.

No sound was audible from the interior, and I supposed that for some reason the preliminaries hadn't begun on schedule. When I got inside, though, I could see two heavyweights in the ring, belaboring each other in a cathedral hush. It was a private fight. The ushers, who at this point outnumbered the customers, treated me with the courtesy that obtains at the best funeral chapels. One waved me to another, each walking a few steps of the way with me. The usher who accompanied me on the final leg showed me my seat, which was indeed in the center of the second row, on the Fiftieth Street side of the ring. There was one man already seated in the row, and the usher suggested to me politely, "If you went around the other way, you wouldn't disturb him." I went around, and found I had the seat next to my fellow patron. It was like the meeting of Robinson Crusoe and Friday. He had been waiting for an audience.

A round ended, and the referee stopped the bout, because one of the men was outclassed. "I could seeyit," my neighbor said. "It was obvious." In the next bout, a fat, pink boy from Florida, who must have been the pride of the boxing coach at some Y.M.C.A., was in with a Negro welterweight who was not inclined to be severe. I fancied I could hear the Florida boy counting to himself, "One-two, one-two," as he hit out nervously. The colored boy would slap him in the belly and push him away. The white boy was off balance constantly, and my expert got the idea that the colored boy was employing some kind of illegal jujitsu on him. "Seeyit?" he would say. "Seeyit? Why don't they get a referee? It's so obvious." The

bout went eight rounds, a tribute to the colored boy's forbearance, and my man was almost tearful with indignation when
the judges gave the colored boy the decision.

The next bout brought together two tough young middleweights from Brooklyn. I had heard of one of them, Ray
Drake, who once beat Floyd Patterson in the amateurs. After
that, Patterson went on to win an Olympic title, and he is a
good professional now. Drake has a choirboy face, wavy hair,
and big, powerful calves—the kind that, when you see them
on a fighter, you know he is going to depend on a lot. Small
torso, big legs, you know he will keep moving. Big torso, short
legs, he has to be a slugger. Big torso *and* big legs, he's a
heavyweight. The other fellow, Rinzy (for Rizzerio) Nocero,
had the big torso. When Nocero came up the aisle, he had
with him Freddie Brown, who had patched Marciano's eye the
night before; Whitey Bimstein, Freddie's partner in the training
and seconding business; and Jimmy Coco, their colleague who
carries the bucket. It was a corner strong enough for a champion, and it indicated that somebody, somewhere, thought
Nocero had a future. It turned out no. They all looked self-
conscious, because they are sociable fellows and they felt
lonely. A cowbell clanged in the obscurity, and a few brave
Brooklyn voices called on Ray and Rinzy. It was the kind of
match that in a small neighborhood club would have produced a near riot. But the few hundred fans who had followed
the boys from Brooklyn were lost in the empty vastnesses. Fight
writers I knew had arrived, and were taking up their posts
behind the typewriter ledges around the ring. I felt sheepish
alone with the expert in the cash section. It looked as if I were
spying on my acquaintances.

At the bell, Nocero rushed in and threw a wicked left hook.
Because of Marciano, all the Italian fighters now want to be
bulls. When Johnny Dundee, fast and flashy, was the Italian
idol, the kids from Italian neighborhoods were all bouncing
off the ropes. Drake would jab Nocero silly, cross the right, hit
him between the eyes with the top of his angelic head, and
then try to tie him up. Seeing Nocero struggling to throw him
off, my expert got the idea that it was jujitsu again. Nocero
was just trying to get his arms free. The public conscience had
found a fellow expert in the row in front of us, which was just

titled him to the peculiar consideration and attention of the *fancy* in general." (I quote from *Boxiana*, the *Mille et Une Nuits* of the London prize ring.) The institution from then on became a resort of the cognoscenti, or knowing coves. Of the Castle while Belcher held the license, Egan wrote, "Propriety is the order of the day, and no man appears more scrupulously exact in exerting his rights as a landlord . . . than Tom Belcher. . . . The inquiring stranger, whom curiosity might have tempted to take a *peep* at the scientific pugilists, feels not the least restraint in visiting the Castle Tavern."

I am reminded of Egan's puff whenever I visit a bar at Eighth Avenue and 55th Street known as the Neutral Corner Cocktail Lounge and Restaurant, Steaks and Chops Our Specialty, Meet Your Favorite Fighters and Managers Here. The Neutral, as its familiars call it, is a few doors north of Stillman's gymnasium and is patronized chiefly by fight managers, trainers, and boxers, who are locked out of Stillman's between three and five o'clock every afternoon, and by ex-boxers, who favor a place where somebody is likely to recognize them. There are two training sessions a day at Stillman's—from noon to three and from five-thirty to seven. The second one is a concession to the economic difficulties now afflicting the Sweet Science; an increasing number of boxers have to hold daytime jobs to keep going, and can work out only after hours. The boxers in the Neutral, being in training, do not drink; they eat on credit and occasionally, when their managers endow them with spending money, play Shuffle Alley, a table game in which one slides metal discs in the direction of electrically controlled tenpins. Because they are temperate and of equable disposition, they seldom raise their voices. The trainers feel constrained to offer an example of sobriety; bottled beer and a cigar are about their speed. The managers are afraid to drink, lest some other manager outwit them, and the ex-boxers are usually too broke to tipple. Any unseemly words that may be heard in the place invariably emanate from some socially insecure sightseer without credentials in any record book. Otherwise, a Belcherian propriety reigns.

The scheme of decoration, like the atmosphere, has a Regency flavor. At the Castle Tavern, Egan wrote, "The numerous sporting subjects, elegantly framed and glazed, have rather an imposing effect upon the entrance of the visitor, among whom may be witnessed animated likenesses of the renowned Jem Belcher [Tom's brother] and his daring competitor, that inordinate glutton, Burke . . . the Champion, Crib, and his tremendous opponent, Molineaux . . . Tom Belcher and his rival, the Jew phenomenon, Dutch Sam . . . with a variety of other subjects, including one of the dog 'Trusty,' the champion of the canine race in fifty battles." The boxers whose likenesses cover the Neutral's walls are of more recent vintages, ranging from John L. Sullivan to one of the bartenders—Tony Janiro, a talented welterweight who retired only a few years ago. The pictures are photographs, instead of hand-tinted engravings, but the faces and torsos are interchangeable with those of 1814. Only Trusty, the champion of the canine race has no opposite number on the Neutral's walls.* Dogfights have gone out of fashion. Janiro has a didactic as well as a utilitarian function; trainers point him out to young fighters as a horrible example. He failed to take his profession with sufficient seriousness, and consequently he never became a champion and is now working union hours. Tony doesn't seem to mind.

I was in the Neutral late one afternoon, enjoying an instructive conversation with Whitey Bimstein, a Mr. Chips of the boxing metier, who was showing me a pound of metal slugs he had confiscated from a pair of his charges, upstate boys, who had intended to use them in coin-box telephones. "They never been away from home before except maybe overnight and they don't want to get homesick," Mr. Bimstein said. "So they bring the slugs along to call their girl friends. Crazy kids. They don't know they can get into trouble that way." He smiled with sympathetic indulgence for youthful sentiment. "Just when their manager gets them a match, they could land in the pokey. 'Write your broad a postcard,' I told them. 'She can wait.'"

Another notable educator present—Charlie Goldman, Rocky Marciano's trainer—said, "One of the troubles with fighters

---

*This is no longer true. A friend outraged at this omission has contributed to the Neutral a photograph of the Dewey Dog, a white bull terrier which won sixty-five fights in and around 1900.

now is they don't start before they're interested in dames. When they used to start at ten, eleven years old, they didn't have the distraction. By the time they did, they knew something." Mr. Goldman, who wears a bowler, bow tie, and chesterfield, in the best tradition of the Jimmy Walker era, is the Beau Brummell, as well as one of the Nestors, of the Neutral. He was a barnstorming flyweight when he was fourteen, fighting feature bouts in places like Savannah, Georgia, and he believes that as the twig is bent, so will be the nose. It is his greatest regret that he didn't get Marciano when Marciano was in about the second grade of public school. "He would have learned to do things right without thinking," Mr. Goldman says. "Then all he would have to think about is what he wanted to do."

These pedagogical reflections were interrupted by a fellow farther along the bar, who was using qualificatives that the bartender on duty—Chickie Bogad—couldn't go along with. Mr. Bogad is one of the three proprietors.

"Excuse me, Jack," Mr. Bogad said, "but you got an awful dirty mouth."

"I don't see no women here," the customer said defiantly.

"There ain't any," Chickie said, "but suppose there was?"

The fellow took this hard. He was a bald, lumpy man with normal ears, and not even a broken nose to make him look at home. "I guess I'm just a qualified hoodlum," he said bitterly. ("Qualified" takes the place of a row of asterisks.)

"If you are," the bartender said severely, "this ain't the joint for you." He moved off toward the beer pumps, under the impression that he had won the argument, but he hadn't. The lumpy man took off his glasses and put them in his pocket.

"Who are *you* to call me a qualified hoodlum?" he yelled after Mr. Bogad.

"You said it yourself," Mr. Bogad replied.

The man yelled, "What business is it of yours, you qualified moralist?"

At that, Mr. Bogad started to come around the end of the bar, grumbling "I don't have to take that from nobody" as he untied his apron, but a squad of gentle young prizefighters formed a wall between him and the customer, while their colleagues shooed the fellow out onto Fifty-fifth Street, explaining that the Neutral was no place for that kind of language.

"See that?" Whitey said. "We got a nice class of kids in the business today. But I sometimes wonder where they going to wind up." This was an allusion to the technological unemployment with which television threatens all boxers who are not already headliners. There is hardly a night of the week now that doesn't offer a nationally televised bout (usually only the main event is shown), and small flesh-and-blood clubs throughout the land have gone out of business because they can't meet this free competition. This condition constantly narrows the opportunity for development of young fighters and—although Whitey isn't so sensitive on the subject—young seconds and trainers. The failure of new stars to emerge is hurting the interests of the television programs themselves—a class isn't in a healthy condition unless it has at least six or eight real contenders—so, as Whitey says, it all adds up to a vicious circle.

The system is taking money even from the star-bout fighters. During the late twenties, the last period of comparable prosperity, Friday-night shows at Madison Square Garden regularly drew from forty to eighty thousand dollars, and each main-bout principal took down from ten to twenty thousand. If the boys weren't fighting at the Garden, they could get almost as much out of town. Now principals in the Garden's Friday-night fights get four thousand dollars each from television, plus a derisory twenty-five per cent of a gate that would have been subnormal in Tiverton, Rhode Island, in 1929—less than five thousand dollars in all. At televised clubs like the St. Nicholas Arena or the Eastern Parkway, they collect about three thousand. In the long view, the best hope for a revival of the dulcet art is that as the television boxing shows run out of new talent, the big and silly television audience will lose interest in them, and national sponsors will let them drop. Then the small clubs will start up again, for the hard core of customers who like boxing well enough to pay for it but who now get it free. This, the cognoscenti say, will insure not only increased employment but a restoration of artistic standards.

"The fellow who used to pay a dollar and a half for a seat in the gallery would never stand for feature bouts like the ones now," an old fighter named Al Thoma, who had stopped by at the Neutral on his way to the Plaza's Oak Room, said. "What you don't pay for, you can't complain about." Thoma, when

fighting, was always known as a cultivated fellow, like Gene
Tunney, but with a faster linguistic change of pace. "The masses
are asses," he said with distaste. "There are no more connois-
seurs. The way most of these guys fight, you'd think they were
two fellows having a fight in a barroom."

Whitey took note of a small, weatherworn taxi-driver, dining
modestly off a short beer and a hard-boiled egg. "Benny Tell,"
Whitey said. "He fought the best. He once fought Pancho
Villa." As Villa died after a fight with Jimmy McLarnin in 1925,
this placed the hackie chronologically. "How many fights you
have, Benny?" Whitey asked.

"About a hundred and fifty," the driver said, pleased at
being recognized. All he had to show for them was a moderately thickened left ear. "They don't make them like Villa no
more," he said. "You hit me and I'll hit you—that's all they
know." He finished his egg and went back to his cab.

"New faces, they want new faces all the time for the television shows," said a trainer named Izzy Blanc, who is younger
than most of the sages, but knowledgeable. "But the new faces
ain't got the experience, so they get knocked out. And where
could they get the experience, with no clubs? Either you got to
rush a prospect or let him starve to death."

If television relinquishes its hold on boxing, and open competition matures a new lot of stars, it is, of course, possible that
the new stars' names will titillate the curiosity of the rumpus-
room audience that sponsors covet. It is also possible that by
then television will have gone the way of such other gadgets as
radio and the silent movies. In the meanwhile young boxers
must live, even though, like modern poets, they have scant
means of communication with the general public. Since the
Guggenheim Foundation has expressed no concern for their
problems, a lot of them run tabs at the Neutral. The tabs are
usually guaranteed by their managers, and since the managers
can't take the money out of the boys until the boys get a fight,
the proprietors of the Neutral show a constructive interest in
any move to re-create the pugilistic equivalent of an off-
Broadway theater. "If we tried to collect now," Nick Masuras,
one of the Neutral's three bosses, said to me, "we would lose
our total clientele."

Masuras is an old middleweight—tough, but not classy—who

used to box in the armories of the New York National Guard in the twenties, when the state permitted the buildings to be used for professional boxing shows on the condition that all participants were Guardsmen. As the required drills were infrequent and there was no prospect of a war, it was a highly successful form of recruiting. Nick's registration card said that he belonged to the 102nd Medical Regiment. After his unspectacular ring career of thirty-eight bouts, he worked in restaurants and then, in 1949, opened the Neutral. He thought of the name himself. Two years later, he pieced the joint up with Bogad, a former matchmaker at the Garden, and with Frankie Jacobs, a veteran fight manager, who contributed social cachet to the establishment.

My visit to the Neutral that particular afternoon was connected with the first attempt by the Metropolitan Boxing Alliance, which consists mostly of managers who hang out in the Neutral, to run a boxing show of its own, with no television, no promoter, no one-sided matches, and—as it turned out—almost no newspaper coverage. For the most part, the members of the Alliance handled young fighters who appeared in preliminaries and semifinals at New York clubs; many of their boys would be fighting features regularly in small cities if television had not blighted the out-of-town spots. The M.B.A.s were in the midst of a highly personal intra-industry feud with the leaders of the International Boxing Guild, a larger and older association of managers, who handle most of the star-bout fighters. The I.B.G.s, according to the M.B.A.s, tried to use their monopoly of the fighters who appear "on top" (in the features) to control employment "underneath" (in the preliminaries). The trainers, like Charlie Goldman and Whitey, were neutral, since they teach and second boys for members of both groups. But they were in favor of any effort to run more fights.

The M.B.A. show, Whitey had informed me, would be a small gem, because in each of the three feature matches scheduled, both the managers concerned figured that they had a shade the better of it. "For a thousand, they might put their kid over his head," Whitey said, "but not for no three hundred." Each of the principals in the three eight-round feature bouts was to receive three hundred dollars, less a hundred for